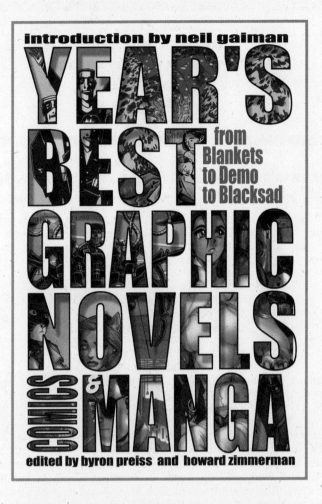

introduction by neil gaiman

YEAR'S
BEST
from
Blankets
to Demo
to Blacksad
GRAPHIC
NOVELS
COMICS & MANGA

edited by byron preiss and howard zimmerman

Edited by BYRON PREISS and HOWARD ZIMMERMAN

Introduction by NEIL GAIMAN

St. Martin's Griffin ≋ New York

DEDICATED TO
THE MEMORY AND VISION
OF BYRON PREISS
1953 – 2005

THE YEAR'S BEST GRAPHIC NOVELS, COMICS, AND MANGA.

Edited by Byron Preiss and HOWARD ZIMMERMAN
Project Coordinator MAUREEN MCTIGUE
Cover design by DEAN MOTTER
Interior design by ARNIE SAWYER

Special thanks to
Christopher Butcher, Jennifer Contino, Jake T. Forbes, Heidi MacDonald and Greg McElhatton
The Guys at Komikwerks.com

Thanks to Shalema McGhee, Max Ulanoff, April Issacs, Paul Levitz, Richard Bruning, Dan Vado, Jennifer de Guzman, Kim Thompson, Eric Reynolds, James Lucas Jones, Chris Staros, Brett Warnock, Eric Shanower, Jim Ottoviani, Steve Leiber, Jeremy Ross, Eric Stephenson, Matt Forsythe, Ted Adams, Neil Kleid, Evelyn Dubocq, Jamie Quail, Peggy Burns, Anders Nilsen, Jessica Able, Larry Young, Chris Pitzer, Paul Hornschemeir, Paul Rivoche, Mark Smylie, Sean Stewart, Steve Bryant, Larry Daley, Allen Hui, and Mark and the gang at Cosmic Comics

For individual copyrights, please see page 270-272.

A BYRON PREISS BOOK

www.stmartins.com

Library of Congress Cataloging-in-Publication Data
Year's Best Graphic Novels, Comics & Manga/edited by Byron Preiss and Howard Zimmerman.
p. cm. "Byron Preiss book."
ISBN: 0-312-34326-4 (pbk)
ISNB-13: 978-0-312-34326-2
ISBN: 0-312-34325-6 (hc)
ISBN-13: 978-0-312-34325-5

1. Graphic Novels

First Edition: December 2005
10 9 8 7 6 5 4 3 2 1

Foreword...........
By Editor Howard Zimmerman

This volume is the result of the combined vision of Marc Resnick, editor at St. Martin's Press and genuine comic-book fan, and the late Byron Preiss, genuine comic-book visionary. And the combined labors of ace co-editor Maureen McTigue and designers Dean Motter and Arnie Sawyer.

The goal of this volume is to expose comics fans to worthwhile areas of the field they may not have yet experienced. Those who spend the majority of their comics-reading time with superheroes will discover that tights-and-fights are not the only enjoyable reads available. Those who focus their attention on Manga should be pleased to see that there are many, many different kinds of stories and formats now available to them. In fact, the comics field is probably more diverse and richer in talent than it has ever been before. And we've drawn work from almost two dozen publishers, independent presses, and self-owned-and-published comics to prove it.

All publishers were invited to participate. Unfortunately, Marvel Comics and Dark Horse Comics declined for their own reasons. Hopefully, they will reconsider and be a presence in next year's volume. And, because of a combination of space limitations and time constraints, such landmark publications as *Cerebus* #300 and the final *Bone* saga are not here, either. Which brings up the question: If it's not here, does that mean it's not among the year's best? And the answer is: Of course not. It would have taken a multi-volume, several-thousand-page series to fully represent the wonderful output of creators and publishers during the past year. Well, not exactly the past year. Given the realities of book publishing, we could not be up to the minute or all-inclusive.

Selections were made from publications that appeared during the period of May 2003 to December 2004. We've parsed down this enormous volume of creative work into three main categories and a fourth catch-all:

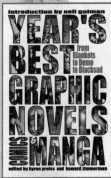

During the course of reading through suggested entries, I rediscovered my love for superhero stories, told well by mature creative teams, and had my eyes opened by the fine work of today's burgeoning field of independent comics producers and self-publishers. I was particularly impressed with *Batman: Hush* and Carla Speed McNeil's work on *Queen and Country*, to name just two.

In addition to reproducing excerpts and cover art from dozens and dozens of periodicals and books, we've also briefly covered the area of web-based comics, where the work keeps getting better and better, stories from comics' anthologies, and several short works. The lengths of the excerpts were driven by several considerations, such as the length of the entire work and the number of entries in that category.

Read on: the thrill of discovery awaits.

discuss the embarrassing mistakes of those who went before them.

Be proud of your mistakes. Well, proud may not be exactly the right word, but respect them, treasure them, be kind to them, learn from them.

And, more than that, and more important than that, make them.

Make mistakes. Make great mistakes, make wonderful mistakes, make glorious mistakes. Better to make a hundred mistakes than to stare at a blank piece of paper too scared to do anything wrong, too scared to do anything.

Critics will grumble. Of course they will. That's one of the functions of critics. As an artist it's your job to give them ulcers, and perhaps even something to get apoplectic about.

Most of the things I've got right over the years, I got right because I'd got them wrong first. It's how we make art.

As a keynote speaker for the Eisners [in 2003] I said that compared to where I dreamed that comics could be, as a young journalist in 1986, we're in a Golden Age.

And I was taken to task in certain circles for this, as if I'd said that this was as good as things could get, or that there was nothing at all wrong with the world of comics. Obviously neither statement is true.

We're in 2004, the year that Dave Sim and Gerhard finished the 300 issues of *Cerebus*, the year that Jeff Smith completed *Bone*, both monumental tasks, both unique. *Cerebus* cannot be compared with anything anyone else has done. It's unparalleled in its evolving portrait of its subject and its subject's creator. *Bone* is, beginning to end, the best fantasy tale anyone's told in comics. That in itself gives me hope for the future.

It's the year that my daughter Maddy discovered *Bettie and Veronica*, and that gives me another kind of hope. Any world in which a nine year old girl can become, off her own bat, a mad keen comics collector because she cares about the stories, is a good one.

I think the Internet is changing things.

Twice in the last eighteen months the Internet has been used as a way of rallying around publishers who needed help. Good publishers with bad cash flow problems, and who put out appeals for assistance, letting people know that now was the time to buy. And people did. The Internet meant that information was given to the people who needed it.

Last week, a web-cartoonist with a large readership, who had told his readership that he would really like to quit his day job and devote the time to the comic, if they could raise the same money he made in his day job. His readers dipped into their pockets, five dollars here and ten dollars

there, and delivered the annual wages from his day job.

The Internet gives your comics cheap access to the world, without printing bills. Of course, it still hasn't worked out a reliable way to pay people for their work, but Randy Milholland quit his job yesterday to do *Something Positive* full-time, and Top Shelf and Fantagraphics are both still here.

Despite the grumblers, I think the Internet is a blessing, not a curse.

And if I have a prediction it's simply this: the often-predicted Death of Comics won't happen. There will be more booms and there will be more busts. Fads and fashions turn up in comics, as with all things, and, as fads and fashions always do, they end, normally in tears.

But comics is a medium, not a fad. It's an art form, not a fashion. The novel was once so called because it was indeed something novel, but it's lasted, and I think, after a few shakedowns, the graphic novel, in whatever form, will do likewise.

Already some things are changing:

When I started writing about comics, before I ever began to write comics, I wanted a world in which comics would simply be regarded as a medium like any other, and in which we were accorded the same respect that any other medium was given. The amount of respect that novels and films and great works of art got. I wanted us to get literary awards. I wanted comics to turn up on the shelves of bookshops, and to sit next to books on the bestseller lists. Maybe one day a comic could come out and be on the *New York Times* bestseller list.

We've got all that. And I don't think it's important after all.

Right now I actually believe that the best thing about comics may well be that it is a gutter medium. We do not know which fork to use, and we eat with our fingers. We are creators of a medium, we create art in an art form, which is still alive, which is powerful, which can do things no other medium can do.

I don't believe that a fraction of the things that can be done with comics have yet been done.

For now, I think we've barely scratched the surface.

And I think that's exciting. I don't know where comics as a medium will go in the future. But I want to be amazed, and I'm pretty sure that I shall be.

And I trust that one day when you, whatever age, race, gender, or ethnicity you may lay claim to, are in your turn a cranky old Jew up here giving a speech, that that will always remain true.

Graphic Novels

By Heidi MacDonald

The timing couldn't be better, really. This inaugural edition of The Year's Best Graphic Novels comes at a time when the form has reached a critical mass much predicted. Setting aside marketing worries that have long preoccupied great minds, the creators of the books gathered here have simply reveled in the power of a medium to tell stories. If there was any doubt that comics—to call them by their dirty, pulp name—are a medium of endless invention, here is the proof.

At one end, baroque tales explore comics' pulp origins. Alan Moore and Kevin O'Neill take familiar heroes and reinvent them with *League of Extraordinary Gentlemen*, while Mark Smylie delivers epic fantasy in a sumptuous style in *Artesia*.

Comics' continuing fascination with hardboiled heroes gets explored in radically different ways. Greg Rucka's spy, Tara Chace, shows her vulnerability in *Queen and Country*. In *Last of the Independents* by Matt Fraction and Keiron Dwyer, one last heist goes wrong, with sepia art paying homage to caper-film roots. *Blacksad* by Juan Diaz Canales and Juanjo Guarnido takes every hardboiled cliché and adds spectacular art and a cast of animals.

Funny animals, a mainstay of comics from *Krazy Kat* to Snoopy, prove that they can be radically unfunny in Jason's extraordinary *You Can't Get There From Here*. Just to prove how different animal characters can be there's *Owly*, Andy Runton's charming little owl.

Moving into art for art's sake, there's *Blab!*, Monte Beauchamp's long running explosion of pop culture sensibility. Bridging the gap between art and story–and showing how far "art" comics have come–there's Anders Nilssen's haunting *Dogs and Water*, a dreamlike tale of a boy and a stuffed bear wandering a wasteland.

Comics have always been a place for the coming-of-age story, and the many directions that theme can go. In *Superman: Secret Identity*, Kurt Busiek and Stuart Immonen take the hoariest of comic book tales and give it human dimension. Dave Gibbons takes his own Mod youth and projects it into *The Originals*, a grim, dystopian future where individuality is a life or death proposition. In the delightful *Scott Pilgrim's Precious Little Life*, Bryan Lee O'Malley pokes fun at his own generation's lack of purpose to make the sitcom no network would dare. Craig Thompson's multi-award winning *Blankets* is a story of first love story that few can resist.

Finally, there are non-fiction comics. In *Suspended in Language* by Jim Ottaviani and Leland Purvis, quantum physics and history come to vivid life with the story of physicist Niels Bohr. Joe Kubert, legendary comics artist, takes on one of the harshest events of human history, with *Yossel*, the story of the doomed Warsaw Ghetto Uprising.

The year's best graphic novels present endless worlds to explore, from campy heroics to fractured fairy tales to the blasted streets of Sarajevo, from Shakespearean superheroes to Victorian mass murderers. Surveying the pleasures to be had here, there is no need for apology or explanation. Just dive right in and see for yourself.

Graphic

Table of Contents

I'm safe.

BLUE REMOTE to **BLUE BASE.** WE HAVE ANOTHER **CONFIRMED.**

NO WORKABLE **PRINTS**--BUT THERE ARE **FINGER GOUGES** IN THE METAL. AND FOOTPRINTS--**DEEP** FOOTPRINTS--NOT ACCOUNTED FOR.

YESSIR. SITE **SECURED.** COLLECTION TEAM **EN ROUTE.**

But it bothers me a little. It used to be more fun.

Just knowing I could do all this, that I was special. It was my secret. My one rare truth, that I knew and nobody else did.

I still like it--I love the flying, I'm glad I can save lives. I'd never give it up.

But something's missing.

KENT! MITTELMARK WANTS YOU IN HER **OFFICE.** NOW.

HUH?

UH, **MA'AM?**

AH, **CLARK.** COME IN, COME IN.

STILL CAN'T GET **OVER** THAT. CLARK KENT. FROM SMALLVILLE, KANSAS, AND YOU'RE A **JOURNALIST.**

NOT **REALLY,** MA'AM.

HM?

I'M A **WRITER**, BUT I DON'T WANT TO BE A REPORTER. AND I'M FROM **PICKETSVILLE.**

SURE, SURE.

UH, DID I DO SOMETHING **WRONG?**

HM? NO, YOUR STAFF WORK IS FINE. I WANT TO TALK ABOUT THIS NEW **PIECE** YOU SUBMITTED.

POPULATION DENSITY AS A MEDIUM FOR BOTH **CULTURAL FERMENT** AND **SOCIETAL DECAY.** INTERESTING. **WELL-OBSERVED.**

I'VE MARKED A FEW SPOTS WHERE THE PROSE IS **UNCLEAR,** BUT I THINK WE CAN BUY IT.

THANK YOU. THAT'S--

YOU HAVE AN UNUSUAL **PERSPECTIVE,** KENT. LIKE YOU SEE THE WORLD FROM **OUTSIDE**--AS A DETACHED OBSERVER, NOT AS A PARTICIPANT.

UH, THANKS **AGAIN.** I TRY TO--

IT WASN'T **WHOLLY** A COMPLIMENT. YOUR WORK ESCAPES **DRYNESS,** BUT STILL, IT'S ALL **HEAD,** NO HEART.

YOU NEED TO GET **OUT** THERE, MIX IT UP. GET **INVOLVED** IN LIFE. GET YOUR HEART BROKEN, GET **LAID. FEEL,** AS WELL AS THINK.

UH....

STILL.... ...ADAM BILMES AT PANTHEON LIKED YOUR EARLIER PIECE, ABOUT GRIDLOCK AS A METAPHOR FOR **INTERNATIONAL DIPLOMACY.**

HE ASKED FOR AN ADVANCE LOOK AT **THIS** ONE. HE'D LIKE TO TALK--SEE IF YOU HAVE A **BOOK** IN YOU.

GIVE HIM A **CALL.**

HE....A **BOOK?**

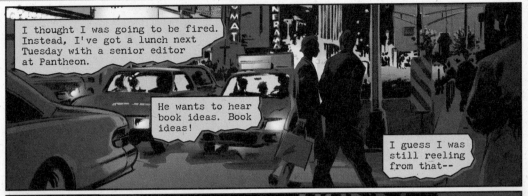

I thought I was going to be fired. Instead, I've got a lunch next Tuesday with a senior editor at Pantheon.

He wants to hear book ideas. Book ideas!

I guess I was still reeling from that--

--and when the guys suggested we all go out for beers and a burger after work, I didn't think.

Didn't realize what they were up to.

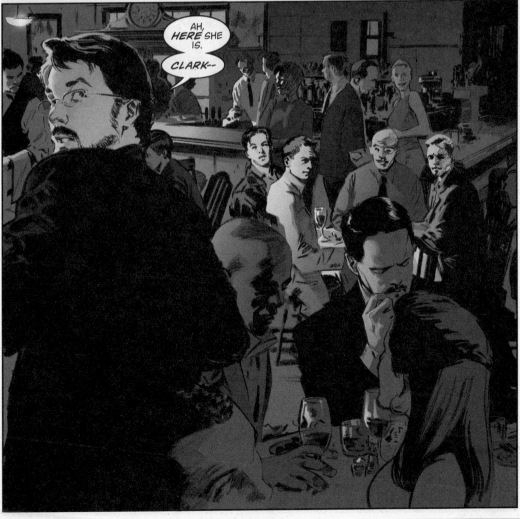

AH, *HERE* SHE IS.

CLARK--

SUPERMAN: SECRET IDENTITY (DC Comics)

--MEET **LOIS**.

HA HA HA HA HA HA HA

GREAT, YOU'VE **HAD** YOUR JOKE. YOU'LL **PAY**, LINDSEY.

HAVE A HELL OF A **NIGHT**.

NICE **WORK** THERE, GUYS. REAL **MATURE**.

AW, **C'MON**, CLARK--

OH, **CHRIST**. NOT **ANOTHER** ONE.

WHAT?

HEY, IT'S **ME**. LOOK, I'D LIKE TO **APOLOGIZE** FOR--

YEAH, YEAH, IT WAS ALL JUST **HARMLESS FUN**, RIGHT?

LISTEN, IF YOU KNEW HOW MANY **TIMES** I'VE--

I mentioned before how much I'm liking Manhattan. Especially at night.

So just let me add this:

It's way, way better when you're sharing it with someone.

She's working for an interior designer. She likes it a lot.

--ALWAYS LIKED TO *WRITE*, BUT WITH THIS NAME, I FIGURE NO NEWS-PAPERS. NOT FOR *ME*.

She's from San Francisco. Went to Carleton College in Minnesota.

She loves Joel Garreau's books too. And she knows Tevis--she's even read The Queen's Gambit!

She wants to go around the world in a balloon someday.

Her nose wrinkles up when she laughs.

And she smiles--

--she smiles like life's a joke, and you're in on it with her.

SO, HOW'D WE *DO?* WORTH ANOTHER TRY SOMETIME?

I'LL HAVE TO GIVE YOU A BUZZ ON THE OL' *SIGNAL WATCH* SOMETIME.

THAT'S JIMMY OLSEN.

WHATEVER.

If I sound smitten, don't read too much into it--

--it's just because I am.

SUPERMAN: SECRET IDENTITY (DC Comics)

BLANKETS (Top Shelf Productions)

Inevitably, a storm would strike and do a number on our ship.

SHATTER the poop deck,

CRUSH the bow,

FLING one bean-stuffed pirate to his fate,

GSSSSH

and FINALLY leave our bed coverings in a state of disarray.

BLANKETS (Top Shelf Productions)

Then we'd gather those crumpled blankets, salvage any remaining crewmates, and wind a nest about us.

The storm would persist all night with waves sloshing the boat and rain gushing down overhead,

But in that little pathetic clump of blankets, there was comfort.

CHSSSHHHH

HHHHHHHHHH

Z

...And surround it with pillows--

FOR CHAIRS.

For dinner, I'd sort through a box of plastic ingredients...

PLAYSKOOL

...and arrange UNIQUE servings:

PIE and an EGG

T-BONE and BANANA

If I was desperate, I'd offer STRAWBERRY SHORTCAKE up for sacrifice.

Unfortunately, none of my invitees were stuffed animals.

Ben and Lauren always showed up; Julie always declined.

And an additional family member at that time was--

I kid you not --

-- A PET MONKEY.

HA HA! As if your household wasn't already a ZOO!

No. I'm serious. He was a CINNAMON CAPUCHIN--

-- and his name was "SNOWBALL".

So he was WHITE?

27

The way she asked questions like that!

I MUST CONFESS, I ADMIRE THE BRITISH PEOPLE'S *BRAVERY.* WITH HORROR AT THEIR DOORSTEP, THEY SEEM *UNCONCERNED.*

Huh. HARDLY *UNCONCERNED.* MORE *BLINKERED,* I'D HAVE SAID.

PRETENDING EVERYTHING'S TICKETY-BOO, NEMO. IT'S THE GREAT BRITISH *PASTIME.*

OUR *DRIVER'S* A DAMNED COWARD, I KNOW THAT MUCH. REFUSING TO GO NEAR THAT SLUG-PIT...

ON THE CONTRARY. HEARING HIM SPEAK TO YOU, I DID NOT THINK HIM COWARDLY.

HOLMES SAID SAMSON WAS A *MAHDI* VETERAN, AND THAT WE SHOULD RE-MAIN *OPTIMISTIC,* AS WE DID THEN.

ACTUALLY, THE MAHDI REVOLT'S A PERFECT EXAMPLE OF ENGLAND'S *COMPLACENCY.* WE WAR-RED ON A CULTURE WE DIDN'T UNDERSTAND...

...AND WE WERE MASSACRED.

I'D ASSUMED HE'D STAYED AT THE *MUSEUM*. HOLMES DIDN'T SPECIFY THAT WE SHOULD *ALL* ACCOMPANY THIS RECONNAISSANCE.

I--I SUPPOSE NOT.

Hunngh. WHAT'S THE POINT OF ALL THIS, IF WE'RE NOT GOING NEAR THAT DAMN CRATER?

PRESUMABLY, WE ARE OBSERVING *CONDITIONS* HERE. THE HAMLET OF MAYBURY, FOR EXAMPLE, IS QUITE *DESERTED...*

WAIT A MINUTE. WHERE'S *GRIFFIN?*

THIS PISSING *STORM'S* GETTING WORSE. LET'S HOPE THAT LITTLE BASTARD'S HORSES DON'T--

What...?

ARRRR!

DRIVER, WHAT ARE YOU *DOING?* YOU ALMOST TURNED US *OVER!*

THAT LAST *LIGHTNING* FLASH. I THOUGHT I SAW SOMETHING!

WH-WHAT'S THAT *NOISE,* BENEATH THE THUNDER? IT'S ALMOST AS IF--

Mr. Griffin?

MR. GRIFFIN, WHAT ARE YOU DOING?

I—I KNOW YOU'RE HERE.

WHY... WHY AREN'T YOU *SAYING* ANYTHING?

GRIFFIN, I DEMAND TO KNOW WHAT'S—

...guu...

Oh!

OHHH!

NO. NO, DON'T...

PLEASE...

AAAA!

NO! LET GO OF—

Whoa!

WHOAHH!

RIGHT. YOU LOT CLIMB OUT. I'LL CARRY ON OVER TO *VAUXHALL* AND REPORT TO *M*.

HE'LL PROBABLY WANT FETCHING BACK HERE TO THE MUSEUM.

NO DOUBT I'LL SEE YOU LATER.

GOD, WHAT A *NIGHTMARE*. THAT BLOODY *MILKING STOOL* THING...

WE'RE ALL IN THE MOST BEASTLY TROUBLE NOW. *ALL* OF US.

LET'S GET INSIDE, OUT OF THIS RAIN.

BUT YOU SAW HOW *FAST* IT MOVED, BOWLING ACROSS THE HORIZON.

A MACHINE LIKE THAT, IT MIGHT BE TOO MUCH EVEN FOR THE *ARMY*...

YOU REALIZE THERE MAY BE A SECOND SUCH DEVICE AT *BYFLEET* ?

OH, GOD. THAT
SURREY *GOLF
LINKS*, WHERE
THE *SECOND*
CYLINDER LANDED.
I'D FORGOTTEN
THAT.

*TWO OF
THEM. AND
WE THOUGHT
THEY COULDN'T
LEAVE THE
CRATER...*

NO. THAT
IS WHAT YOU
ENGLISH
ASSUMED. I
THOUGHT OTHER-
WISE...

YES. YES, YOU SAID
THEY'D BE BUILDING
SOME SORT OF
VEHICLE.

WHILE WE WERE ALL
HOPING FOR THE BEST, YOU
WERE EXPECTING THE
WORST.

It is as
you stated.
To hope for
the best is
an English
failing.

Grow-
ing up in
Mombai, in
calcutta, one
learns dif-'
ferently...

SCOTT PILGRIM (Oni Press)

SCOTT PILGRIM (Oni Press)

MATTHEW PATEL WAS THE ONLY NON-WHITE, NON-JOCK KID IN SCHOOL, PROBABLY THE ONLY ONE FOR MILES AROUND, OR IN THE ENTIRE STATE, FOR ALL I KNOW. SO, OF COURSE...

KISSY KISSY

WE JOINED FORCES AND TOOK 'EM ALL OUT. WE WERE ONE HELL OF A TEAM. NOTHING COULD BEAT MATTHEW'S MYSTICAL POWERS COMBINED WITH MY BRUTE STRENGTH.

NOTHING BUT PRE-ADOLESCENT CAPRICIOUSNESS.

BLAB! (Fantagraphics)

A CHARLOTTE, N.C. LAWYER PURCHASED A BOX OF VERY RARE AND EXPENSIVE CIGARS...

...THEN INSURED THEM AGAINST FIRE, AMONG OTHER THINGS...

...WITHIN A MONTH, HAVING SMOKED HIS ENTIRE STOCKPILE OF THESE CIGARS...

...AND WITHOUT YET HAVING MADE EVEN HIS FIRST PREMIUM PAYMENT...

...THE LAWYER FILED CLAIM AGAINST THE INSURANCE COMPANY, SEEKING RECOMPENSE...

...FOR THE DESTRUCTION OF THE INSURED ITEMS IN A "SERIES OF SMALL FIRES'...

...THE INSURANCE COMPANY REFUSED TO PAY, CITING THE OBVIOUS REASON...

...THAT THE MAN HAD CONSUMED THE CIGARS IN THE NORMAL FASHION. THE LAWYER SUED, AND WON!

IN DELIVERING THE RULING THE JUDGE AGREED WITH THE INSURANCE COMPANY THAT THE CLAIM WAS FRIVOLOUS, BUT STATED NEVERTHELESS, THAT THE LAWYER HELD A POLICY IN WHICH THE COMPANY WARRANTED THAT THE CIGARS WERE INSURABLE AGAINST FIRE WITHOUT DEFINING WHAT IS CONSIDERED TO BE UNACCEPTABLE FIRE, AND THUS WAS OBLIGATED TO PAY THE CLAIM.

RATHER THAN ENDURE A LENGTHY, COSTLY APPEAL PROCESS...

...THE INSURANCE COMPANY PAID $15,000 TO THE LAWYER FOR HIS LOSS...

...AFTER THE LAWYER CASHED THE CHECK, THE COMPANY HAD HIM ARRESTED ON...

...24 COUNTS OF ARSON! THE LAWYER WAS CONVICTED OF INTENTIONALLY BURNING...

...PROPERTY AND SENTENCED TO 24 MONTHS IN JAIL AND A $24,000 FINE.

BLAB! (Fantagraphics)

No obvious signs of trauma. He appears to have died in his sleep.

You have a cause?

I'll need an autopsy to be sure, of course.

But if I had to guess, I'd say it was a cerebral hemorrhage of some sort...or perhaps an aneurysm.

His right pupil is exploded, which is consistent with that finding.

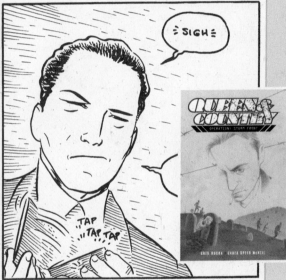

It's a pity. He's quite young.

He's twenty-six.

≥ SIGH ≥

TAP TAP TAP

When will you move him?

When we're done.

It's just that we're busy this week, this room was supposed to be ready for--

When we're DONE.

British embassy, please.

Thank you.

QUEEN AND COUNTRY (Oni Press)

CALL CAME FROM THE FCO OFFICE, VIA THE EMBASSY IN CARACAS.

HE WAS DISCOVERED THIS MORNING, IN HIS HOTEL ROOM, IN HIS BED.

THE CARACAS POLICE ARE INVESTIGATING.

DO THEY... I MEAN, DO WE... ED WAS ONLY SUPPOSED TO *BACK UP* THE STATION ON THE LAUGHLIN SURVEILLANCE.

THAT'S **ALL** HE WAS DOING, RIGHT?

THAT'S **ALL** HE WAS DOING, TOM.

THE DUTY OPS OFFICER GOT A SIGNAL LAST NIGHT SAYING THEY'D WRAPPED UP, ED WAS SUPPOSED TO MAKE HIS WAY HOME TODAY.

CARACAS STATION CONFIRMS HE'D FINISHED. **THEY'D** FINISHED.

HOW?

WE DON'T *KNOW.* I'VE SENT THE CARACAS NUMBER TWO, JANICE O'HARE, OUT TO MAKE INQUIRIES. RIGHT NOW, THE POLICE ARE SAYING IT LOOKS LIKE ED DIED IN HIS SLEEP.

THEY'LL DO AN AUTOPSY. WE'LL KNOW MORE THEN.

BOLLOCKS.

I WAS HIS HEAD OF SECTION. *I* SHOULD DO IT.

ALL RIGHT, BUT **NOT** YET.

NOT UNTIL WE KNOW WHEN WE'RE GETTING THE **BODY** BACK.

FIRST THING TOMORROW, I WANT YOU TO HEAD OUT TO THE **SCHOOL**, SEE IF THERE'S A **REPLACEMENT** FOR ED IN **TRAINING**.

WE'RE PLUCKING A **VIRGIN**?

NO CHOICE.

THERE'S NO ONE IN **ROSTER** SLATED FOR **SPECIAL OPERATIONS**.

IS THERE ANYTHING *I* CAN DO?

YOU CAN **CLEAR** OUT ED'S **DESK**.

E. KITTERIN

I'VE GOT TO INFORM C AND THE DEPUTY CHIEF.

"THE LINE'S" TRAIN STATION WAS A LOYAL REFLECTION OF ITS NEIGHBORHOOD. AN IMAGE OF WHAT IT COULD HAVE BEEN BUT NEVER WAS. TEN YEARS AGO, THE CONSTRUCTION OF THE SITE HAD STOPPED, LEAVING IT HALF BUILT. ALONG WITH THE FACTORIES CLOSED BECAUSE OF THE CRISIS, IT TOOK PART IN THE GHOSTLY SCENERY OF THIS SUBURB.

WEEKLY HAD DISAPPEARED, AND DON'T ASK ME WHY, BUT DESPITE IT ALL, I KIND OF MISSED HIS "FINE SMELL."

SO I DECIDED TO FOLLOW THE MAGPIE, WHO I THOUGHT WAS A LOT LESS INNOCENT THAN HE APPEARED TO BE.

HOW MUCH WILL YOU GIVE ME FOR THIS?

WHERE'S THE OWNER OF THAT CAMERA?

I DON'T KNOW WHAT YOU'RE TALKING ABOUT, MISTER...

I'M TALKING ABOUT MY FRIEND, THE REPORTER. I'M AFRAID HE'S BEEN KIDNAPPED AND YOU MIGHT KNOW WHERE HE IS.

AND WHAT'S YOUR ROLE IN ALL THIS? YOU'VE BEEN FOLLOWING ME SINCE THE DAY I STEPPED FOOT IN THIS STINKING PLACE. YOU'RE A DAMN BIRD OF ILL OMEN.

I DON'T KNOW ANYTHING. THEY NEVER TELL ME ANYTHING.

THEY?

I'M JUST A POOR DEVIL WHO ONLY WANTS TO LIVE LONG ENOUGH TO GET TO GO TO LAS VEGAS...

YOU LIKE TO GAMBLE, HUH? OK, OLD MAN, LET'S PLAY A LITTLE GAME: I ASK QUESTIONS AND YOU ANSWER!

OK! I'LL TAKE YOU TO HIM! JUST DON'T KILL ME, I BEG YOU!

WHERE ARE "THEY" HIDING MY FRIEND? ANSWER ME!

LET'S GO. TIME IS RUNNING OUT.

TELL ME THAT THERE'S NOTHING BETWEEN YOU AND HUK.

I'M SURPRISED YOU EVEN PAID ATTENTION TO THAT JERK. YOU KNOW BETTER THAN ANYONE THAT I'D NEVER LET ANY MAN TOUCH ME. IT DISGUSTS ME WAY TOO MUCH!

GOD, JEZZ! IT'S UNBEARABLE TO THINK THAT SOMEONE ELSE IS ENJOYING WHAT I'VE BEEN DENIED FOR SO LONG...

OH, CALM DOWN HANS! YOU KNEW EXACTLY WHAT WAS IN STORE FOR YOU WHEN WE ARRANGED OUR MARRIAGE. ANYWAY, IT LOOKS LIKE YOU'VE FOUND SOMEONE TO CONSOLE YOU, HAVEN'T YOU?

I MEAN, THOSE CHOIR KIDS TO WHOM YOU ARE SO DEVOTED...

...OH!

DON'T YOU DARE EVER REPEAT WHAT YOU'VE JUST SAID! YOU KNOW THAT'S AN INFAMOUS LIE!

WHAT WOULD YOU DO? MAKE A SCENE BY THROWING ME OUT OF THE HOUSE, LIKE YOU DID WITH YOUR FIRST WIFE? NO. UNFORTUNATELY FOR YOU, I'M NOT SOME POOR BLACK GIRL LIKE SHE WAS.

I KNOW THIS PLACE LIKE THE PALM OF MY HAND. I USED TO WORK HERE WHEN IT WAS THE BIGGEST PLANE FACTORY IN THE COUNTRY. I COULD MOVE THROUGH IT WITH MY EYES CLOSED! HA-HA!

GLOSMUL AIRCRAFT INDUSTRIES NO TRESPASSING

IT WAS THE ONLY THING I COULD DO TO SERVE MY COUNTRY. I COULDN'T JOIN IN COMBAT BECAUSE OF MY BEING BLIND AND ALL.

AND I WOULD HAVE PREFERRED TO NEVER TO HAVE SEEN WHAT I SAW OVER THERE.

WHERE WERE YOU POSTED? IN EUROPE? I WOULD'VE LIKED TO BE A PILOT.

IRONIC ISN'T IT ? A BIRD WHO CAN'T FLY.

IT'S NOT THE FIRST TIME THAT A VERMIN LIKE YOU LEAD ME TO A TRAP, YOU KNOW, COTTEN...

TROMP!

...COTTEN?

YOU CAN'T GET THERE FROM HERE (Fantagraphics)

YOU CAN'T GET THERE FROM HERE (Fantagraphics)

THE WAR IN EUROPE DIDN'T SLOW NUCLEAR PHYSICS RESEARCH APPRECIABLY —ESPECIALLY SINCE SO MANY TOP PHYSICISTS HAD HEADED *WEST.* **OTTO FRISCH** AND **RUDOLPH PEIERLS✱** HAD SETTLED IN *ENGLAND* WHILE OTHERS, LIKE **FERMI** AND **EINSTEIN** BEFORE THEM, ENDED UP IN THE *U.S.*

BUT THE WAR **DID** LEND SOME *URGENCY* TO THAT RESEARCH, EVEN THOUGH THE PREDOMINANT VIEW WAS STILL MUCH LIKE **RUTHERFORD'S** IN 1933:

ONE TIMELY WORD OF WARNING IS ISSUED TO THOSE WHO LOOK FOR SOURCES OF POWER IN ATOMIC TRANSMUTATIONS — —SUCH EXPECTATIONS ARE THE MEREST *MOONSHINE.*

BOHR *SHARED* THIS VIEW, THOUGH FOR *ENGINEERING* RATHER THAN SCIENTIFIC/THEORETICAL REASONS.

LISTEN, **TELLER.** THE AMERICANS ESTIMATE THAT IT WILL TAKE THEM 10 DAYS OF AROUND-THE-CLOCK OPERATION TO SEPARATE ONE THOUSAND MILLIONTH OF A *GRAM* OF **U-235** FROM RAW URANIUM ORE.

WHY, YOU'D HAVE TO TURN THE *WHOLE COUNTRY* INTO A *FACTORY* TO MAKE ANY PROGRESS AT ALL!

ABOUT A MONTH AFTER **FRISCH** AND **PEIERLS** MADE PUBLIC THEIR CALCULATIONS ON THE CRITICAL MASS OF **U-235** NEEDED FOR A *BOMB* — IT WAS *NOT TONS,* BUT IT *WAS* A LOT MORE THAN ONE THOUSAND MILLIONTH OF A GRAM! — *GERMANY* OCCUPIED *DENMARK* TO ENSURE THAT THE COUNTRY WOULD "ACCEPT THE PROTECTION OF THE REICH."

✱ RUDOLPH E. PEIERLS WAS (YET ANOTHER) OF *BOHR'S* COLLABORATORS. A TOP-NOTCH MATHEMATICIAN, A REFUGEE ... AND THE AUTHOR OF "*THE ATOM THAT BOHR BUILT.*"

BOHR HAD JUST COME FROM *NORWAY*, WHERE HE HAD REPORTED ON THE CONFIRMATION OF HIS U-235 THEORY.

UPON HIS RETURN TO *COPENHAGEN*, HE WAS EFFECTIVELY UNDER HOUSE ARREST.

MESSAGES URGING BOHR TO *LEAVE IMMEDIATELY* BEGAN TO ARRIVE AT THE INSTITUTE. WITH A JEWISH MOTHER AND THEIR WORK ON PLACING REFUGEE INTELLECTUALS WELL KNOWN, NIELS, HARALD AND THEIR FAMILIES WERE TARGETS.

BUT THEY DECIDED TO STAY, SINCE THE BOHR BROTHERS WERE ALSO SYMBOLS OF *DANISH CULTURE* IN THE FACE OF NAZI EFFORTS TO ESTABLISH DOMINANCE. NOT SO MUCH BY PHYSICAL MEANS (YET), BUT MORE SUBTLY.

WERNER. WHY HAVE YOU COME?

PROFESSOR, SO GOOD OF YOU TO HAVE ME.

AND SO THEY TALKED, JUST AS THEY HAD IN THE PAST. AND....NOT JUST LIKE IN THE PAST, FOR **HEISENBERG** HAD STAYED IN *GERMANY* AND IN DOING SO HAD — IN THE MINDS OF MANY — TACITLY ENDORSED THE NAZIS. HE SAW IT DIFFERENTLY, OF COURSE.

DID HE HAVE *CALCULATIONS*?

IF YOU HAVE CALCULATIONS—WELL, YOU KNOW THAT'S NOT HOW I...

AND I WOULD BE ASHAMED TO KNOW THAT IT'S HOW YOU WOULD APPROACH...

DID HE HAVE A *MESSAGE* FOR **BOHR?**

IF IT'S A LETTER TO ME, *TELL* ME WHAT IT SAYS. HERE. NOW, WE WILL DISCUSS THINGS.

BUT IF YOU WANT ME TO PASS ALONG SOMETHING TO OTHERS, I...

I NEED HARDLY STRESS THAT I CAN'T BE A MESSENGER, *FOR YOU*, UNDER THESE CIRCUMSTANCES.

WAS THERE EVEN A PIECE OF PAPER *AT ALL*? WHAT HAPPENED IS **UN-CLEAR** TO THIS DAY, SINCE NEITHER SPOKE OF THEIR MEETING IN DETAIL TO ANYONE.

AND THEY WERE ALONE IN THE WOODS.

205

THE REMAINS

I AM THE QUEEN OF DARA DESS.

I AM THE QUEEN OF A BROKEN CITADEL TWO HUNDRED AND FIFTY MILES AWAY ACROSS HILL AND DALE AND CRAG.

I HAVE SAID SO, AND MEN AND WOMEN HAVE BELIEVED ME.

LET THEM KNOW WE'RE HERE.

LET LOOSE!

INDEED, I THINK SOME BELIEVED I WAS A QUEEN BEFORE I DID.

ARTESIA (Archaia Studio Press)

I PRICK UP MY EARS, AND LISTEN TO THE SPIRITS AT PLAY ON THE WINDS.

THEY BRING ME THE BABBLE OF AN EMPIRE...

...TONGUES AND DIALECTS APLENTY.

BUT MY MOTHER'S ART CAN MAKE THEM CLEAR.

ARTESIA (Archaia Studio Press)

GRAPHIC NOVELS

ARTESIA (Archaia Studio Press)

ARTESIA (Archaia Studio Press)

ARTESIA (Archaia Studio Press)

THOUGH PERHAPS NOT BY THEIR *ABSENCE.*

WE HAVE HAD A CHANCE TO TAKE THE MEASURE OF OUR ALLIES.

THE FORCES WE HAVE WITH US WILL STAND WELL IN BATTLE TOMORROW.

BUT THE THESSIDS...

AYE. THE *THESSIDS.*

THE THESSIDS SCARE ME.

THIS CAMPAIGN IS TOO WELL PLANNED, AND THERE ARE TOO MANY OF THEM.

AND WE HAVEN'T EVEN SEEN THEIR MAIN HOST YET.

THE ISLIKLIDS SCARE ME.

THE ISLIKLID SCARES ME.

I CAN'T BELIEVE THERE'S ONLY ONE OF THEM LURKING IN THEIR HOST...

...OR WHAT IT DID TO OUR CAMP.

THEN THERE ARE THE PRISONERS TO CONSIDER.

BETWEEN OUR VARIOUS CAMPS, WE'VE CLOSE TO *TWO THOUSAND* OF THEM.

WE CAN'T FEED THEM ALL.

...AND IF THEY RECOVER THEIR WITS, AND SEE HOW *FEW* HOLD THEM...

TWO THOUSAND THESSID PRISONERS BEHIND US.

THREE THOUSAND THESSIDS IN FRONT OF US.

MAY THE MORNING STAR BRING US A WAY TO BE RID OF *BOTH.*

ARTESIA (Archaia Studio Press)

I DON'T KNOW WHY THE REBBE'S DEATH STRUCK ME SO HARD. DEATH AND DYING WERE ALL AROUND ME EVERY WAKING HOUR OF THE DAY. ON THE STREETS LAY THE BODIES OF THOSE WHO COULD NO LONGER STAND. IGNORED, THEY WAITED PATIENTLY, QUIETLY, FOR THE CREAKING CART TO COME BY AND PICK THEM UP. THEN, TO BE THROWN ON LIKE A SACK OF LOOSE BONES, PILED ONTO THE CHALKY BODIES BENEATH.

BUT, THE REBBE HAD SURVIVED THE FIRE. ESCAPED THE CAMP. ELUDED PUNISHMENT AND DEATH TO SNEAK INTO THE GHETTO. TO BE ABSORBED INTO THE ONLY PLACE HE FELT SAFE. WITH HIS PEOPLE.

OH, THE IRONY. THE SADNESS OF IT ALL.

"HIS DEATH MUST BE MARKED, MORDECAI. IT MUST NOT GO UNNOTICED."

"HOW DO YOU PROPOSE THAT SHOULD BE DONE, YOSSEL?"

Joe Kubert

yossel

April 19 1943

THE NEXT MORNING, I APPROACHED THE GREY WALLS OF THE SECURITY POLICE BUILDING. THE SKY WAS SMUDGED WITH BLACK SMOKE RISING FROM BUILDINGS ALREADY REDUCED TO RUBBLE AND BURNING.

OUR CAPTORS WERE HERDING THE GHETTO'S REMNANT OCCUPANTS INTO TIGHTER GROUPS BY REDUCING THE HABITABLE AREAS WITH RELENTLESS PRECISION.

YOSSEL (ibooks inc.)

I PLACED MY CAP UNDER MY CHAIR.

NOTHING EXISTED FOR ME EXCEPT MY DRAWINGS THAT SEEMED TO FLOW FROM MY PENCIL. I FELT A NUMBNESS, A PRESSURE JUST ABOVE AND BEHIND MY EYES.

HOW THEY LAUGHED AND JOKED AT THE PICTURES I DREW. THEY WERE AMUSED BY THE MUSCULAR HEROES. "TRUE NAZIS", THEY SAID. "RULERS OF THE WORLD."

"LOOK HOW THE LITTLE JEW DRAWS."

"THE PENCIL— IT MOVES SO FAST."

"IT IS A GIFT. HE IS SO LUCKY."

I DID NOT LOOK BACK AS I WALKED AWAY FROM THE BUILDING. FROM MY AUDIENCE OF SMILING, JOKING ADMIRERS. THEIR LAUGHTER FADED WITH EVERY STEP I TOOK AWAY FROM THAT HATED PLACE.

THEN THE EXPLOSION ERUPTED. IT WAS DEAFENING. I FELT THE BLAST ACROSS MY BACK, LIKE A GIANT HAND SHOVING ME. PIECES OF DEBRIS FELL AROUND ME... AT MY FEET... ON MY SHOULDER. STILL, I DID NOT LOOK BACK.

BEFORE I LEFT I HAD TAKEN MY CAP FROM UNDER MY CHAIR AND REPLACED IT WITH TWO ARMED GRENADES I'D HIDDEN IN MY JACKET POCKETS. I HAD ONLY SECONDS TO LEAVE THE BUILDING.

I LOOKED STRAIGHT AHEAD, BUT I SAW NOTHING. ONLY THE FACES OF THOSE WHO LIVED YET IN MY MIND. MAMA... PAPA... MY SISTER, CHAIYA... AND THE REBBE.

REPRISAL WAS INEVITABLE AND IMMINENT. IT
BEGAN IN APRIL. ON THE SECOND NIGHT OF
PASSOVER.

A GERMAN REINFORCEMENT OF TWO THOUSAND
SOLDIERS ENTERED THE GHETTO. THEIR MISSION
WAS CLEAR. MORE BUILDINGS WERE BOMBED
AND SET AFIRE. THE DEAD AND THE DYING WERE
SCATTERED EVERYWHERE. THOSE WHO COULD
STILL MOVE WERE PACKED ON TRUCKS AND
TRANSPORTED OUT. CHAOS UNFETTERED
ROAMED THE SCARRED STREETS.

THOSE WHO ATTEMPTED TO
EVADE OR ESCAPE WERE
INSTANTLY MURDERED IN
MID-FLIGHT. THE OLD, THE
LAME, THE SICK,... BABIES
IN THEIR MOTHER'S ARMS.
NONE WERE SPARED.

YOSSEL (ibooks inc.)

AT 6 AM, ON THE NINETEENTH OF APRIL, 1943, THE GERMAN ASSAULT ON THE WARSAW GHETTO BEGAN.

AT DAWN, WE WERE ON THE ROOF OF OUR BUILDING. EACH OF US CARRIED GUNS, AMMUNITION, GRENADES, KNIVES. ALL WE HAD TAKEN FROM THE SOLDIERS' DEAD BODIES.

A SMOKY HAZE LAY ON THE MORNING AIR, DIMMING THE WEAK SUNLIGHT. THEN WE HEARD THE CLANK AND GRIND OF METAL TREADS AS TANKS APPROACHED THE GHETTO WALL. NOW WE COULD SEE THEM. THE SWASTIKA-ADORNED ARMORED JUGGERNAUTS AND THE SOLDIERS, ROW UPON ROW, MARCHING INTO THE GHETTO.

"I HAVE NEVER SEEN SO MANY SOLDIERS, MORDECAI."

"THAT WILL MAKE EASIER TARGETS FOR US, YOSSEL."

"THEY ARE... COMING INTO... OUR BUILDING."

OWLY (Top Shelf Productions)

OWLY (Top Shelf Productions)

THE ORIGINALS (Vertigo/DC Comics)

The Originals.

THE ORIGINALS (Vertigo/DC Comics)

THE ORIGINALS (Vertigo/DC Comics)

Comics
By Greg McElhatton

Single issues of comics are simultaneously the backbone of the comics industry and an endangered species. There's no denying that for over half a century the periodical form has been the delivery standard. Bags, boards, and long boxes are the tools of the collector's trade, and you can buy specially quality-graded and sealed issues from companies whose sole purpose is to determine the level of a comic's pristine condition. Most comic specialty stores gain the bulk of their profits—and pay the rent—through the selling of periodicals.

But the rise of graphic novels as a market force has shifted attention away from the traditional monthly format. Deciding to wait for a collected edition is now the rule for many rather than the exception. Additionally, many publishers have abandoned or heavily shifted away from single issues of comics.

The sad thing is that, even as all of this occurs, some of the most exciting comics published in the last year are in this original format. Joss Whedon, John Cassaday, and Laura Martin's *The Astonishing X-Men* was a regular dose of pure excitement, introducing new villains and reviving old characters in 32-page installments. In many ways, their first six-issue storyline could be used as a primer on how to craft a popular ongoing comic. It's also hard to argue against the strength of a book as perfect as Eric Shanower's *Age of Bronze*. A retelling of the Trojan War, every issue features iconic covers that pop off the stands, and meticulously crafted interior art that is as lush and provocative as the story it's presenting.

Bringing old characters and stories to life is a trait more often seen in periodicals than graphic novels. From the unexpectedly fantastic revival of *Conan* by Kurt Busiek and Cary Nord, to Kyle Baker's crazy take on *Plastic Man*, periodicals can be used as a testing ground to see if the market is ready to see familiar faces again. A project like Darwyn Cooke's 400-page DC: *The New Frontier* might have been daunting to potential customers, but in six 64-page installments it's easier to give it a chance.

Periodicals can build up momentum and excitement for an "event." Books like *Identity Crisis*, showing up over seven months, were able to get reactions out of readers in a way that a single volume couldn't.

Last but not least, periodicals are a place for slightly different, off-beat, or more obscure titles to experiment and build an audience. You can use the format to tell stories about a homeless skateboarding girl who fights ninjas, or twelve unconnected tales of super-powered teenagers, or an American expatriate living in Mexico City, or an aboriginal tracker who makes his way through life in a world containing elements of both our past and future. Jim Rugg and Brian Maruca's *Street Angel*, Brian Wood and Becky Cloonan's *Demo*, Jessica Abel's *La Perdida*, and Carla Speed McNeil's *Finder* are all books that were able to gain

Table of Contents

buzz and popularity over time through serialization even as their creators continued to shape and refine their craft. While all these books have "graphic novel collections" published or scheduled, it was through their initial editions as periodicals that they were able to make a splash.

Graphic novels may be the wave of the future, but the comics in this book will show you that there are still great things to be found in this time-honored format.

STREET ANGEL (Slave Labor Graphics)

IRRITATED, STREET ANGEL TRIUMPHANTLY SURVEYS THE WAREHOUSE.

WHERE'S MY SHOE?

STREET ANGEL (Slave Labor Graphics)

Lay out yer cards, pardner. What's yer big line? Betcha got an ace up yer sleeve...

Umm... all right... How's... ummm...

Er, no, WAIT! YEAH! How's thi-- No, no, that's dumb. Hold on. Umm...

Oh, COME ON, man!

You can DO this!

AGE OF BRONZE (Image Comics/Hungry Tiger Press)

151

AGE OF BRONZE (Image Comics/Hungry Tiger Press)

YES...

...FOR TROY TO FALL, THE FIRST-BORN DAUGHTER OF AGAMEMNON MUST DIE.

I'M BOUND BY HONOR TO RESCUE HER IF SHE ASKS ME TO, MOTHER.

IF YOU RESCUE HER, YOU WON'T SAIL FOR TROY. THAT'S WHAT I'VE WANTED ALL ALONG... BUT NOW -- I FEAR A BATTLE AT THE ALTAR.

MOTHER, DEATH LIES IN WAIT FOR *EVERYONE*.

YOUR DEATH WILL COME FROM THE SUN GOD IN RETRIBUTION FOR YOUR SLAYING A SON OF HIS.

I HAVEN'T SLAIN ONE YET.

I CAN MAKE SURE YOU NEVER DO.

MNEMON, COME HERE.

AGE OF BRONZE (Image Comics/Hungry Tiger Press)

MNEMON CAN RECOGNIZE THE SUN GOD'S CHILDREN. FROM NOW ON HE'LL ACCOMPANY YOU INTO BATTLE TO STEER YOU AWAY FROM EVERY SON OF THE GOD.

CAN YOU FIGHT, MNEMON?

I'LL FIGHT WELL FOR YOU, SON OF THE NEREID, AND KEEP YOU SAFE.

VERY GOOD ANSWER.

THEN PUT ON ARMOR AND GET READY FOR BATTLE.

BUT WE WON'T FACE THE SUN GOD TONIGHT. THE GIRL IS CLAIMED BY ARTEMIS OF THE HUNT, THE MOON GODDESS.

TAKE MY BLESSING WITH YOU, ALL OF YOU...

THANK YOU, MOTHER.

LET'S GO!

...AND REMEMBER THAT THE SUN GOD ALWAYS FOLLOWS HIS SISTER, THE MOON.

MONDAY, OCTOBER 18, 1999

IT.

AH... THE OLD BITCH.

SORRY?

SOME OF MY COLLEAGUES ARE A LITTLE *SUPERSTITIOUS* ABOUT THE BROOKLYN BRIDGE. IT'S ALWAYS BEEN BAD LUCK FOR CIVIL ENGINEERS.

POLICE

THE ONE WHO DESIGNED IT DIED FROM *TETANUS* AFTER AN ACCIDENT ON THE PILINGS. AND HIS SON GOT A FATAL CASE OF THE *BENDS* FROM WORKING UNDERWATER ON THE--

--FOUNDATIONS?

YEAH, THAT'S WHERE I SAW SOMETHING *GLOWING.*

WHAT?

AND YOU DIDN'T CALL THE *BOMB SQUAD?* OR THE--

I WORKED DEMOLITIONS FOR NINE YEARS, SIR. THIS AIN'T A BOMB. BESIDES, IT'S NOT *ATTACHED* TO THE BRIDGE, LOOKS MORE LIKE IT'S GROWING *OUT* OF IT.

HERE, TAKE A LOOK FOR YOUR-SELF...

PATROLMAN RICK A BRADBURY

NEW YORK CITY N° 2

EX MACHINA (Wildstorm Productions)

DEMO (AiT/Planet Lar)

NAH, THESE ARE THE OLD ONES. ALL THEY DO IS MAKE YOU SWEAT. ANY DECENT SHOT FROM AN *AK'LL* GO RIGHT THROUGH IT.

BETTER TO NOT HAVE IT AND STAY ON YOUR TOES THAN TRUST IT TO SAVE YOUR LIFE.

WE SHOULD BE GETTING THE NEW ONES *"ANY DAY NOW."*

CLANG

YOUR BEST DEFENSE IS A STRONG OFFENSE ANYWAY. JUST KEEP YOUR EYES *PEELED* FOR INCOMING VEHICLES.

ANY CAR COMING HERE KNOWS TO STOP. THEY SEE THE SIGNS, THEY SEE THE BARRIER, AND THEY SEE US POINTING OUR WEAPONS. THEY KNOW THEY GOTTA *STOP.*

IF THEY *DON'T STOP,* WE GOTTA ASSUME IT'S HOSTILE AND THEY GOT WEAPONS, MAYBE A BOMB. WE SHOOT FIRST, WE TAKE 'EM OUT.

WHAT, LIKE, DISABLE THE VEHICLE?

NO, FUCKHEAD, SHOOT TO *KILL.* TAKE THE WHOLE FUCKING THING OUT.

THAT'S WHY YOU'RE HERE, AIN'T IT?

BESIDES, I HEAR YOU ARE ONE *HOT-SHIT* SHOT, YOU *NEVER* MISS.

SOME KINDA BORN-WITH-A-RIFLE-IN-HIS-HAND FARM BOY?

YEAH, SOMETHING LIKE THAT. I DON'T MISS TOO OFTEN.

I HEAR YOU DON'T MISS *EVER.*

YEAH, NOT TOO OFTEN, NO.

THEY RECRUITED ME PRETTY HARD BECAUSE OF IT. MY HIGH SCHOOL COACH GAVE THEM MY NUMBER. HE USED TO HUNT WITH ME AND MY OLD MAN.

SO WHAT WAS IT THAT GOT YOU? THE "EARN AN EXTRA PAYCHECK?" OR THE "ONE WEEKEND A MONTH?"

"EARN MONEY FOR COLLEGE." IT'S THE ONLY WAY I CAN AFFORD IT.

COPY THAT, "CITIZEN-SOLDIER." I THOUGHT I'D BE PUTTING OUT FOREST FIRES AND DRIVING HUMVEES AROUND, NOT SWEATING LIKE A *FUCKING PIG* HALFWAY AROUND THE WORLD FOR THE LAST SIX MONTHS.

NO SHIT, ME TOO.

COLLEGE BETTER BE FUCKING WORTH IT.

HE'S STOPPING.

WHAT THE FUCK? COME ON! COME ON!

WHAT DO YOU THINK IT MEANS?

MAYBE SCARED, MAYBE NOT...

HATFIELD! YOU HANG BACK AND COVER US.

OH, FUCK.

VREEEEEEE

DEMO (AiT/Planet Lar)

FABLES (Vertigo/DC Comics)

5 am... the "speculum darkroom" nightclub.

SHERIFF LOIS McCREEDY C.P.D.

YUP.

...so the guy turned into a vampire or whatever and tess shot at him with this big stupid holy water cannon she made. but that just sorta pissed him off worse so, um... well, i dunno why i thought of a pony right then, but that's what i conjured up. it swallowed him whole and he's still in there, i guess.

that pony's not very sturdy, though. it'll start to dissolve in about an hour or so.

YEAH, WELL IT'S AN SSI* PROBLEM NOW.

serenity rose

HOME OF THE HEART SHAPED SKULL

THEY'LL BE HERE WITHIN THE HOUR.

OUR BUDDY HERE GETS LOOSE BEFORE THEN, WE GOT ENOUGH SILVER-TIP ROUNDS IN HERE TO LIGHT THAT SUCKER UP LIKE A TIFFANY'S DISPLAY.

I'D JUST AS SOON PUT HIM OUTTA HIS MISERY RIGHT NOW, BUT YOU KNOW HOW THE FEDS ARE.

yeah... ...but maybe they can, um... y'know... fix... him.

...YOU'RE SHITTIN' ME, RIGHT?

uh...

*ssi = supernatural shield initiative. sort of the fbi of spookystuff.

SERENITY ROSE (Slave Labor Graphics)

REPORTS COMING IN

CHAOS IN CRESTFALLEN

POLICE CALLED TO **THIS** LATE-NIGHT DANCE CLUB

SO-CALLED "GOTHIC" UNDERGROUND

DETAILS SKETCHY AT THE MOMENT

APPARENT **VAMPIRE** ATTACK

23-YEAR-OLD **MICHAEL STATTEN**

OVERDOSE

"THAT BOY... I ALWAYS KNOWED..."

"8-FOOT **BLEEP**ING PONY..."

WE'RE NOW READY TO

CONFIRMING THE INVOLVE-MENT OF MS. SERENITY ELIZABETH ROSE

PERHAPS BEST KNOWN FOR **HIJACKING** A SCHOOL BUS AT THE AGE OF

SINGLE-HANDEDLY TOOK ON A WHOLE **PLATOON** OF SSI SHOCK TROOPS

NEVER LIVED IT D-

BUT JUST WHAT **WAS** HER ROLE IN THIS, THIS...

DANGEROUS

SATANIC

TERRORIST

MONSTER

SERENITY ROSE (Slave Labor Graphics)

SERENITY ROSE (Slave Labor Graphics)

there are five american witches.
i don't really know any of them.
i don't really know any other witches.

i met atlan samuel when i was about 3 years old.
i guess. i don't remember him at all. he and that
canadian witch came to the house one time to
convince my parents to "let the government help
raise me." my dad threw them out.

my dad
was neat.

emily ash is another one.
she's about 40 years old or so, a homemaker.
a hardcore christian homemaker, "church of right thinking." her
denomination doesn't take kindly to any of this supernatural funny
business. as far as i know, she's never so much as floated a pencil.

people don't talk about ogden michael falmouth too much
anymore, except when they're trying to make a point about how dangerous
we witchy types are. he and his girlfriend went on a bit of a
rampage back in the 50's, blasting their way across seven
states until a federal sniper finally put a bullet in his
skull. he's been comatose and under lockdown ever since.

TERROR
COUPLE
KILLS

then
there's
me.
some people
think i oughtta
be locked up, too...

but the most famous american
witch of the moment, maybe even more
famous than atlan samuel, is marvin garden,*
aka "rivet hed." marvin liked to play with corpses
when he was a kid. now he plays with steel,
lightning, and ectoplasm on stage most every
night as part of his traveling freak show.

builds up nightmares and breaks
them down to the delight of
children the world over...

*the kind of name you just can't make up.

SERENITY ROSE (Slave Labor Graphics)

KRASH

I'M GETTING OUTTA HERE. GET MY MONEY BACK.

ALL UNITS! GET SOME HELP DOWN HERE!

GO AHEAD. FOLLOW ME.

I HAVEN'T EATEN SINCE LUNCH.

TRESHHH

I DON'T LIKE THIS.

I DON'T LIKE YOU.

No one seriously injured. The guards will get double hazard pay. And Croc has escaped.

So far, so good.

THAT'S ALL RIGHT. I'M NOT HERE TO BE LIKED.

I DON'T NEED TO REMIND YOU THAT THE *FATHER* OF THE *BOY* THAT... *BEAST*...KIDNAPPED IS A *PERSONAL* FRIEND OF THE PRESIDENT.

Amanda Waller heads up President Luthor's Office of Meta-Human Affairs.

I have history with Waller. None of it pleasant.

That's all right. I'm not here to be liked either.

Dealing with anything remotely connected to Luthor makes my skin crawl. But, Croc was about to be transferred out of my city...

YOU MEAN HE'S A *MAJOR* CONTRIBUTOR TO *LUTHOR'S* CAMPAIGN PARTY.

YOU'VE GOT UNTIL *MIDNIGHT.*

THEN, CROC IS *OURS.*

KRAKA THOOM

MASTER BRUCE...?

GO AHEAD, ALFRED.

A CAR JUST PULLED UP TO THE HOUSE. ARE WE EXPECTING COMPANY?

NO.

PHILADELPHIA LICENSE PLATE. HMX 19...I CAN'T MAKE OUT THE LAST NUMBER IN THIS STORM.

I have until midnight...

WENT TO THE MOVIES THE OTHER NIGHT WITH JOE FROM WORK AND HIS COUSIN LOUIE FROM BELL GARDENS. CRACKING ME UP WITH THEIR USUAL BICKERING AND SPECIAL BRAND OF CHICANO UNHUMOR.

Life through whispers
by Xaime 2004

THE INCREDIBLE SHRINKING MAN

AFTER THE MOVIE THE GUYS WEREN'T READY TO HEAD HOME JUST YET SO WE POPPED INTO CHEETAH TORPEDA'S FOR A NIGHTCAP AND A LITTLE POOCHIE.

I HADN'T BEEN THERE FOR SOME TIME, EVER SINCE MY FAVORITE DANCER AND OVERALL HEARTBREAKER, THE LOVELY VELVET, OR VIVIAN I GUESS IS HER REAL NAME, DISAPPEARED. JUST WHEN I GOT TO KNOW HER TOO.

LOVE AND ROCKETS
NO. 10

COME TO THINK OF IT, I HADN'T SEEN ANYBODY IN SOME TIME. EVER SINCE DOYLE CAME OUT AND TRIED TO GIVE ME THAT HUMMER WHEN WE WERE BOTH SCHNOCKERED. THINGS SLOWED DOWN QUITE A BIT. MAYBE HE'S EMBARRASSED ABOUT IT, I DUNNO, MAYBE IT'S ME.

THEN LIKE A LARK, THIS ONE BLONDE WHO SITS DOWN WITH US TURNS OUT TO BE ONE OF DOYLE'S GANG FROM THAT DIVE ON LAS PALMAS AND ASKS ME WHY I'M NOT OVER THERE WITH EVERYBODY CELEBRATING ITS LAST NIGHT OPEN.

ALL I KNOW IS 'EVERYBODY' BETTER MEAN VIVIAN SO I ASK THE GUYS IF THEY WANT TO HIT IT UP BUT THEY'RE TOO BUSY HITTING THE BLONDE UP FOR LAP DANCES SO I LEFT WITHOUT THEIR SORRY ASSES.

SO, WAS SHE GONNA REMEMBER ME? I MEAN, WE ONLY TALKED ONCE. AND WHAT IF SHE'S WITH THAT SLIMY MOBSTER GUY SID? WHAT IF SHE'S NOT EVEN THERE?? WHAT IF...? SHIT, I'M TOO OLD FOR THIS.

TOO OLD TO BE HOPPING AROUND TOWN IN PURSUIT OF A PRETTY GIRL. TOO OLD TO BE WASTING TIME NOT BEING IN PURSUIT OF THIS PRETTY GIRL. TOO OLD PERIOD. THEN AGAIN, WHAT ELSE SHOULD I BE WASTING MY TIME ON?

SO THE PLACE IS PACKED. I DON'T SEE DOYLE OR VIVIAN BUT THERE'S THAT CRAZY SILENT FUCKER, THE ONE THEY CALL BORNEO, BEATING THE HOLY SHIT OUT OF SOME POOR BASTARD. I CAN SEE THE FUN HAS ALREADY STARTED.

TEN MINUTES AND I HAD IT. VIV OR NO VIV, I DECIDED TO JET BEFORE I RAN INTO MY OWN BULLSHIT. SO THEN, I'M NOT TWO FEET FROM THE EXIT AND BLAM! THERE IT IS. MY HEART JOLTED BUT I STILL MANAGED TO MAKE IT OUTSIDE.

DAMN, WAS IT REALLY HER? WAS IT MAGGIE? MAGGIE WITH DIFFERENT HAIR? WHAT THE HELL WAS SHE DOING HERE? WELL, I KNOW SHE KNOWS DOYLE, BUT... DOES SHE KNOW VIVIAN, TOO? FUCK, DID SHE NOTICE ME? SHE LOOKED RIGHT AT ME! MY GOD, WHAT'S NEXT?

I'LL TELL YOU WHAT'S NEXT. VIVACIOUS VIV AND SLIMY SID, THAT'S WHAT. THEY SEEMED TO BE IN PRIVATE CONVERSATION. BEFORE I COULD SLIP BACK INTO THE BAR, THEY SPOTTED ME AND VIVIAN SAID HI.

I SAID HI BACK BUT BEFORE I COULD ESCAPE SHE CALLED ME OVER IN THAT FOGHORN VOICE OF HERS. ON ANY OTHER OCCASION IT WOULD BE HEAVEN BUT AT THIS MOMENT I WANTED TO GO HOME AND HIDE UNDER MY BED.

SHE ASKED ME HOW I'D BEEN LIKE WE WERE OLD PALS. I COULDN'T TELL, WAS I SAVING HER FROM THAT SLIME WHO JUST KEPT GLARING AT ME LIKE HE WAS STUDYING MY FACE SO HE'D KNOW WHO TO HAVE KILLED LATER?

HATE TO ADMIT IT, BUT AS MUCH AS I'D LOVE TO BE HER KNIGHT IN SHINING ARMOR, I WANTED TO GET THE HELL OUT OF THERE MUCH MORE. I TOLD HER I HAD TO PEE BUT THAT I'D SEE HER INSIDE. PURDY SMOOVE, EH?

THEN I MADE MY SMOOVE EXIT (WHICH WAS MORE LIKE A FAST MOTION SCENE FROM GILLIGAN'S ISLAND) BUT I WENT IN THE WRONG DIRECTION AND ENDED UP RIGHT AROUND THE CORNER DEAD ENDED IN A FLOWER BED.

I DIDN'T DARE MOVE, HOPING THEY WOULD THINK I TOOK OFF DOWN THE STREET. I COULD STILL HEAR THEIR VOICES BUT COULDN'T MAKE OUT THEIR CONVERSATION. I THINK THEY WERE ARGUING ABOUT FOLK ART.

③

THERE I WAS, TRAPPED IN THIS STUPID, FUCKING SITUATION WHEN I COULD HAVE BEEN SITTING WITH BORING OL' JOE FROM WORK AND HIS COUSIN LOUIE WITH THEIR CRUMMY JOKES WATCHING POOCHIE.

THEN I THOUGHT ABOUT SEEING MAGGIE. I HADN'T SEEN HER IN SO LONG. GOD, SHE WAS BEAUTIFUL. SHE'S LIKE, THIS WOMAN NOW. THIS... JUST WHEN YOU THINK YOU GOT IT ALL FIGURED OUT... MAN O MAN.

BUT THEN I STARTED THINKING ABOUT HOW WE SHOULD HAVE NEVER BROKE UP AND ALL THAT SHIT BUT BEFORE I COULD BLAME THE WHOLE WORLD FOR MY BITTERNESS, I HEARD SOME RUDE SOUNDS AROUND THE CORNER.

I SWORE SID WAS HURTING VIVIAN BUT WHEN I DARTED OUT TO TRY AND STOP IT THEY WERE NOT THERE. BUT FURTHER DOWN THE WAY WAS DOYLE. HE WAS WATCHING SOMETHING GOING ON IN THE PARKING LOT.

IT LOOKED LIKE THE GUY BORNEO AND ANOTHER GUY WERE HELPING SOMEONE INTO A CAR. BUT BEFORE I COULD SEE MORE, DOYLE BLOCKED MY VIEW AND ASKED ME WHERE THE FUCK MY SAGGY ASS HAS BEEN.

I ASKED HIM WHAT WAS UP AND HE SAID SOME ASSBITE GOT TOO DRUNK AND THEY WERE TAKING HIM HOME. I GET IT, FIRST, BLOODY UP THE GUY AND THEN NURSE HIS WOUNDS. THEN DOYLE TOOK ME IN TO BUY ME A DRINK AND ASKED IF I'D SEEN VIVIAN YET.

SHE WAS SITTING INSIDE BY HERSELF. I ASKED DOYLE IF THAT SID FUCK WAS STILL AROUND AND HE JUST LAUGHED AND SAID, "THE FUCKER'S MARRIED." I'M NOT SURE WHAT THAT MEANT BUT I FELT A LITTLE EASIER TO SIT WITH HER.

THERE SHE WAS, STICKIN' STICKIN' STICKIN' BUT NOW SHE WASN'T TALKING. DOYLE SAID HE'D GO GET MY DRINK AND THEN SHOT ME THAT 'GO FOR IT' GLANCE BEFORE HE LEFT. JUST LIKE THE FUCKER USED TO DO IN HIGH SCHOOL.

SHE AND I SAT THERE FOR AWHILE NOT TALKING. THEN JUST WHEN I WAS ABOUT TO ASK HER IF SHE KNEW MAGGIE, SHE DECIDED TO SPEAK. FROGMOUTH LIKE, SHE ASKED ME WHY I WEAR A SUIT.

I DECIDED TO BE CHARMING AND USE AN OLD STANDBY. I SAID THAT EVERY ONCE IN AWHILE A MAN OUGHT TO WEAR A SUIT. IT WENT NOWHERE. SHEESH, IMAGINE IF SHE KNEW THE JACKET AND PANTS DIDN'T EVEN MATCH.

THEN DOYLE CAME BACK AND RIGHT AWAY HE ASKED ME IF I COULD TAKE VIVIAN HOME LATER. I SHRUGGED, THEN HE GAVE HER THE 'BEHAVE YOURSELF' LOOK. I STARTED TO FEEL LIKE I WAS BEING SET UP, BUT NOT FOR A DATE.

THE NEXT HALF HOUR I SPENT IN THAT BAR WAS JUST PLAIN WEIRD. PEOPLE COMING IN AND OUT. A LOT OF WHISPERING BACK AND FORTH. AND WHERE DID MAGGIE GO? I NEED SOMEONE NORMAL AROUND.

LOVE AND ROCKETS (Fantagraphics)

THEN IT WAS TIME TO GO. DOYLE WALKED OUT WITH US. HE TOLD ME I WAS A GALLANT KNIGHT FOR DRIVING VIVIAN HOME. I TOLD HIM TO SUCK MY DICK. THEN I SAID, NEVER MIND. THINGS GOT NORMAL FOR A SECOND.

THEN I SAW THE GUY, OR I THINK IT WAS THE GUY THAT BORNEO BEAT THE FUCK OUT OF. DID HE COME BACK FOR MORE? HE REALLY DIDN'T SEEM THAT DRUNK. I DUNNO, IT GOT REAL STRANGE ALL OVER AGAIN.

THEN I SAW IT. THE PUDDLE OF BLOOD IN THE PARKING LOT AND SOMETHING CLICKED IN MY HEAD AND I GOT A COLD CHILL. THEN I SWEAR I HEARD DOYLE SAY UNDER HIS BREATH, "THOSE FUCKERS WENT AND DID IT."

I LOOKED AT HIM AND HE HAD THE SADDEST LOOK ON HIS FACE, THEN IT CHANGED AS HE LOOKED AT ME LIKE WE BOTH KNEW SOMETHING, THEN HE SAID TO MAKE SURE VIV GETS HOME OK AND THEN HE WAS GONE.

AS I DROVE VIVIAN HOME SHE STARTED TO OPEN UP. SHE ASKED ME IF I KNEW A GIRL NAMED MAGGIE. I DON'T KNOW WHY BUT I JUST SAID "YEAH, THROUGH DOYLE." SHE SIGHED AND SAID, "EVERYTHING'S THROUGH DOYLE."

BUT I WASN'T REALLY LISTENING. ALL I COULD DO WAS PICTURE SOMEONE'S FUCKED UP DEAD BODY LAYING SOMEWHERE IN THE L.A. RIVER. THEN I WONDERED WHERE JOE AND LOUIE WERE, CRUMMY JOKES AND ALL.

THE END

LA PERDIDA (Fantagraphics)

LA PERDIDA (Fantagraphics)

HSU AND CHAN (Slave Labor Graphics)

BY ALL THAT'S HOLY-- THIS MUST STOP!

CHAN! CHAN! LOOK... AT... THIS!

IT... UM... IT LOOKS LIKE A TOOTHBRUSH.

IT'S MY TOOTHBRUSH!

...IT LOOKS FINE.

TAKE A WHIFF.

SHORTLY...

WE'VE FACED HORRORS IN OUR LIVES BEFORE-- DEATHS IN THE FAMILY, AWKWARD DATING SITUATIONS, "ERIN BROCKOVICH," UNSIGHTLY RASHES, A TRIP TO FRANCE--

BUT THIS... THIS NIGHTMARE OF DEMONIC SHENANIGANS MUST BE BROUGHT TO A HALT!

MY NOSTRILS.. BURNING.. :GACK!:

BY ALL THE VARIED AND OFTEN INEFFECTUAL FORCES OF GOODNESS AND LIGHT IN THIS WORLD, WE MUST WAGE A WAR ON HELL ITSELF!

OR, AT LEAST, THE REPRESENTATIVES THEREOF WHICH ARE CURRENTLY SULPHUR-ING UP THE LIVING ROOM!

TO ARMS!

WH-- WHAT ARE WE GOING TO DO?

WE'RE GOING TO DESTROY THE FORCES OF EVIL.

OKAY, I SUPPOSE I SORT OF MEANT, "HOW ARE WE GOING TO DO THIS?"

OH.

I DUNNO, HIT THEM WITH STUFF, I GUESS.

WE DID GET THOSE RUBBER MALLETS A WHILE AGO, AND NEVER GOT A CHANCE TO USE 'EM...

DON'T YOU THINK WE MIGHT WANT TO FIND SOME WEAPONS THAT ARE A BIT MORE... SPIRITUAL IN NATURE?

OH, SURE, CHAN -- LET'S JUST HOLD A SEANCE AND SEE IF WE CAN'T SUMMON THE ETERNAL SOUL OF A BLACKJACK OR SOMETHING, VERY INTELLIGENT.

NOW COME HELP ME LOOK FOR THE BB RIFLE.

I MEAN THE BOOK, HSU! IF IT BROUGHT THEM HERE, MAYBE IT CAN GET RID OF THEM, TOO!

HMM... WELL, WE'LL HAVE TO HIT 'EM WITH IT PRETTY HARD...

COMICS

HSU AND CHAN (Slave Labor Graphics)

203

HSU AND CHAN (Slave Labor Graphics)

COMICS

HSU AND CHAN (Slave Labor Graphics)

Manga

By Jake T. Forbes

Ever since the "manga boom" took the publishing world by storm in 2002, people have been searching for the secret to manga's success. In principle, *manga* is just the Japanese word for comics. The concept of telling stories through sequential art transcends language and nationality, and while the tools and techniques used by Japanese *manga-ka* and Western comics artists differ, both are more alike than different. The business and consumption of manga, however, is so fundamentally different from American comics as to dwarf their similarities. Manga really is ubiquitous in Japan and read by people of all ages and walks of life. It's cheap, convenient, and disposable, thanks to the "phone book" anthologies for which most manga is created. And because manga is so universally accepted in Japan, the market can support incredible diversity of subjects and styles.

The role that manga plays in Japan is much like cable television here. Instead of channels, anthologies cater to specific tastes and demographics. In addition to the high-school-romance and action-themed books, there are anthologies specializing in mystery, fantasy or horror for genre enthusiasts; "Office Lady" and "Salaryman" anthologies for white-collar workers; and there are entire magazines dedicated to just golf, pachinko (a kind of pinball-gambling), and the tile game Mah-Jongg. The collected editions, or *tankobon*, are the equivalents of DVDs in that they feature better quality printing and are books one tends to keep.

It was only when U.S. publishers stopped trying to fit manga into the failing comic book mold and adopted something closer to the Japanese system that manga really took off over here. Cheaper prices, a smaller trim size and a more "authentic" presentation—complete with right-to-left reading order— were all key to manga's triple digit growth. More important, however, was the willingness to embrace manga's diversity and publish series that didn't fit the model expected from comics.

One of the earliest success stories in American manga publishing is the work of CLAMP, the prolific four-woman studio. The group's ability to switch art styles and genres, from the baroque and apocalyptic *X/1999* to the wispy romance *Wish* won them fans of both genders and helped redefine (for better or worse) what manga looked like to the mainstream. To this day, their crossover hit *Chobits*, a bittersweet sci-fi romance, is a "gateway drug" for new manga readers.

Long the backbone of the boys manga in Japan, *Shonen Jump* is leading the way for new action titles in America. With over a half dozen series currently running on TV taken from the *Shonen Jump* imprint, as well as video games, toys, and apparel, this is manga at its most mainstream. But as the brand matures, we're starting to see less-traditional boys fare work its way in. Who would have

Table of Contents

guessed five years ago that *Hikaru no Go*, a series about a ghost teaching a boy the secrets of an ancient board game, would sell to kids in America?

Shojo (girls) manga has been the most talked about category as it opened the world's eyes to the fact that *gasp!* girls will read comics. Whereas *shonen* (boys) manga tends to focus on goal-based conflict (overcoming the external forces or personal demons necessary to win the game or beat the bad guys), shojo manga tends to be more about enduring the constant barrage of emotions that defines being a teenager. Sometimes the situations feel painfully real, other times they're wickedly excessive. Often they're both at the same time, as is the case with *Hot Gimmick*. The story of a high-school-age girl who gets blackmailed into becoming the personal slave of the cold-hearted (but cute!) boy next door keeps the emotional level turned up, yet keeps the characters sympathetic to the reader.

While it is teen-friendly fare that dominates manga sales in America, there remains a trickle of classic series that showcase the best of manga as an art form. At the top of anyone's manga reading list should be the work of Osamu Tezuka. His work has been getting new attention in translation thanks to the recent releases of *Astro Boy*, *Phoenix*, and *Buddha*. There's a reason why any manga creator you ask will list him as in influence—no one else in Japan, if not the world, understood as well as he the emotional and narrative potential of the sequential-art medium.

Manga represents a path that comics could have taken in America, if over the past few decades the format hadn't developed the stigma of being for nerdy guys and kids. Slowly but surely the comics industry is working to change perceptions. In the meantime, there's no rush—there's plenty of great content to read from Japan!

Manga

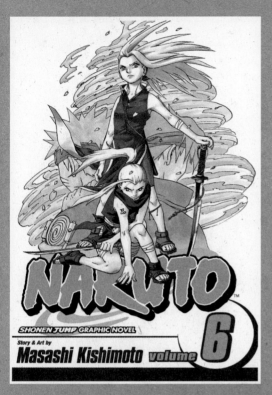

SHONEN JUMP GRAPHIC NOVEL

Story & Art by
Masashi Kishimoto volume 6

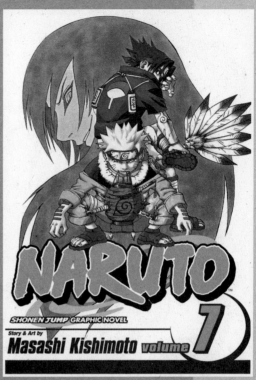

SHONEN JUMP GRAPHIC NOVEL

Story & Art by
Masashi Kishimoto volume 7

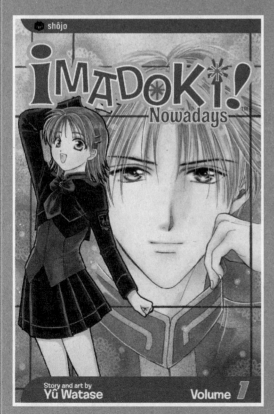

shôjo

IMADOKI!
Nowadays

Story and art by
Yû Watase   Volume 1

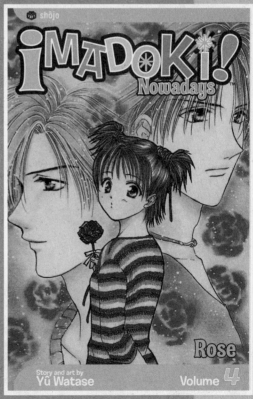

shôjo

IMADOKI!
Nowadays

Rose

Story and art by
Yû Watase   Volume 4

AI!

AND, YES, I KNOW YOU DIDN'T KNOW I WAS WAITING...

AI, I'VE BEEN WAITING FOR YOU-- YOU REALLY HAD ME WORRIED!

YOU CAN'T DO THIS TO ME. SOMETHING ABOUT YOU... YOU'RE NOT LIKE ANYONE I'VE EVER MET.

KENT, LET ME GO. THIS IS ALREADY HARD ENOUGH ON ME.

HM?

OH, NOW I SEE--YOU THINK YOU'RE HER DUDE!

GIVE IT UP!

......

DON'T BE A DOG WHO CHASES SPEEDING CARS...

...YOU'LL JUST GET YOURSELF RUN OVER.

LET'S GO!

KOFFFR

MY POOR BABY...

SIZZLE

WHAT IS THAT THING?!

Her dragon wings spit fire!

I DON'T KNOW! BACK IN MY WORLD, SHE'S CALLED A FURIE. NOT TOO POPULAR WITH THE GUYS...

WE'VE GOT TO GET TO A STREET WHERE WE CAN FIND SOME PEOPLE...

NO WAY! WE'LL JUST BE RISKING THEIR LIVES!

GOT A BETTER PLAN?!

LET HIRA TAKE YOUR WORRIES AWAY, PRINCESS.

YOU CAN TRUST US.

.....

LET GO!

WHACK

KENT--

YOU'RE MINE NOW!

GOTCHA! NOW YOU'RE COMING WITH ME!

AGH!

AI!

I'VE NEVER BEEN ANYONE'S BEFORE--

PRINCESS AI (TokyoPop)

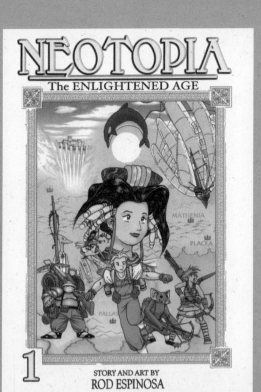

NEOTOPIA
The ENLIGHTENED AGE

1

STORY AND ART BY
ROD ESPINOSA

NEOTOPIA
The PERILOUS WINDS of ATHANON

2

STORY AND ART BY
ROD ESPINOSA

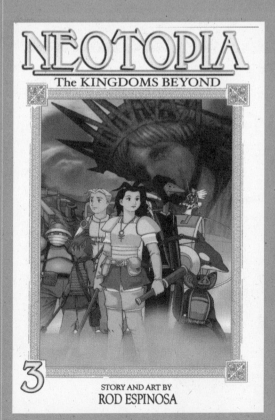

NEOTOPIA
The KINGDOMS BEYOND

3

STORY AND ART BY
ROD ESPINOSA

LEGENDS FROM
DARKWOOD

THE UNICORN HUNTERS
By CHRISTOPHER REID & JOHN KANTZ

AKIHITO YOSHITOMI

One of the great things about the comics medium is that it provides the ability to experiment. Whether that be with storytelling, with art style, with the size of the book, the type of paper, or going digital; whether it be the chance to move past the traditional superhero story and tell a story about a family, about growing up and old, or about technology run rampant, or all of the above in a single tale, comics offer a whole other scale of reach beyond traditional print books.

Our "Best of the Rest" section showcases this. The content is eclectic: anthologies, web comics, ashcans, small press, major publisher, self-published, Xeric-associated. A little bit of everything.

Just like comics.

The Internet, as Neil Gaiman states in his introduction, has become a broad and sturdy base for comics. Internet campaigns to save publishers have succeeded. Digital comics can be found in all shapes, sizes, styles and stories, and provide a daily, weekly or monthly respite for surfers everywhere. The two spotlighted here are Eisner-nominated... but there are so many others worth a look, beyond those graced with awards and nominations. They run the gamut from politics, to farce, to personal, to whatever-comes-to-mind. What ashcans used to be, digital comics have become and moved well-beyond.

Ashcans, the one-dollar or two-dollar photocopied comics, are still very much around. The "sampler" showcase of a larger publication, or a portfolio, or the classic mini-comic are still abundant at comic book conventions across North America. The sample spotlighted here, *Family Reunion*, exists as a self-contained story, as all good comics should, but also as an introduction to the novel *Perfect Circle*; the main character in the comic is the main character of the novel. He now lives and breathes as more than just words on the page; he is real, as real as pencil and ink and imagination will allow.

There's a cynical axiom of publishing that anthologies just won't sell, that if you give readers a collection of material by a variety of talented people, they won't go for it. Readers want, it's believed, one book driven by one person. And certainly many book buyers do routinely avoid anthologies. But, oh, what they're missing. *Sandman* became and still is a phenomena all its own—an original short-story book, telling tales of all the Endless, can do nothing but sell well.

Table of Contents

A name writer and a group of big-name artists working on known characters is saleable and will fly off the shelves; that it happens to be good is just a bonus. We've ended the book with *Sandman* in a "bookend" fashion: Gaiman's prose lead us in, and his storytelling brings us out. The other anthology noted here is *Project: Telstar*, with a themed approach—robots in space, in this case. The book is a fantastic cross-section of potent indy talent.

Ninety Candles started out as an experiment—tell a story by creating a panel or a page to reflect each passing day. The Xeric-Award winning project shifted a bit and became a "life story" following one man's dream and life. Because in comics, you can see someone's life flash right before your eyes. Some of the other projects, like *American Elf*, *Farewell Georgia* and others are more than worth your time. They reflect life and passion and talent and the belief that what you have to say matters. They may not fall into specific categories, but these project still reflect and represent the best talent and tales the field has to offer.

DALY • BRYANT • FIDLER™

ATHENA VOLTAIRE

UPDATED MONDAY, WEDNESDAY AND FRIDAY
WWW.ATHENAVOLTAIRE.COM

by matthew forsythe

ROBOT IN THE RAIN

I CAME ACROSS HIM BY CHANCE, HUNCHED IN THE DAMP CHILL OF THE WEST LOWER 4020 LEVEL. SLEEPLESS, BEHIND IN MY WORK, LOOKING FOR CHANCE INSPIRATION, I WAS ON ONE OF MY NIGHTLY WANDERS THROUGH THE MILES OF FORGOTTEN ALLEYWAYS AND TECHNOGUTTERS BENEATH THE CITY...

AT FIRST GLANCE, HE LOOKED EXACTLY THE SAME AS ANY ONE OF THE FIFTY THOUSAND OTHER BEGGARBOTS WHICH LITTER THE CITY...

I NEVER USED TO STOP FOR THESE PESTILENT, BROKEN MACHINES. I HAD MY JOB, MY WORRIES, MY DEADLINES. I HAD ENOUGH OF A LOAD!

BESIDES, I COULD NOT SAVE THEM ALL. WHAT GOOD WOULD STOPPING HAVE DONE?

I NEVER STOPPED---

...BUT THIS TIME I DID.

HE TOLD ME OF HOW MEN, IN A DESPERATE ATTEMPT TO SURVIVE, TO PREVAIL, TOOK TO WEARING METAL SKINS, TURNING THEMSELVES INTO ROBOTS, ACQUIRING VAST POWERS BEYOND THE HUMAN...

BUT ALL THIS WAS NOT ENOUGH TO DEFEAT THE INVADERS. THE ALIENS KILLED ALL....SAVE FOR A FEW, SAVE FOR THE HIDDEN ONES.

AND THEN, INEXPLICABLY, AFTER PLUNDERING THE EMPIRE, THEY SIMPLY LEFT, SATED...

I ASKED WHEN ALL THIS HAD HAPPENED, AND HE SAID: "200 CENTURIES AGO."

I ASKED WHO HE WAS, AND HOW HE CAME TO KNOW THESE MANY THINGS...

HE REPLIED, "I WAS THEIR LEADER, AND A MAN SUCH AS YOU."

"I WAS THEIR PROTECTOR AND THEIR KING, AND IN ALL THE TIME SINCE, I HAVE WANDERED THE GLOBE, SURVIVING, SEARCHING FOR OUR LOST WEAPONS, FEARING THE INVADERS' RETURN...

IT WAS ALL TOO FANTASTIC; I BEGAN TO LAUGH ALMOST INVOLUNTARILY, SHUDDERING IN THE COLD.

IT WAS UTTERLY *IMPOSSIBLE!*

THE WORLD WAS FULL OF ROBOTS, YES; AND MANY WERE DESTITUTE BEGGARS. BUT NONE WERE IMMORTAL, THE FALLEN KINGS OF LONG-VANISHED EMPIRES!

UNDAUNTED, HE MADE HIS APPEAL: TIME IS SHORT---WOULD I HELP HIM, SINCE HIS FRAME WAS WEAKENED, TO FIND ANY OF HIS SURVIVING LOST BRETHREN, HIS SUBJECTS... TO ASSEMBLE, TO ORGANIZE.... TO PREPARE?

I REMEMBER IT ALL SO WELL, THAT MOMENT, NOW AND FOREVER...THE CONSTANT DAMP CHILL, THE DISTANT HUSH OF THE HOVERWAYS, THE SMELL OF ANCIENT METAL...

...BUT GOD HELP ME, I LAUGHED AGAIN, AND SAID: *"PREPARE FOR WHAT?"*

237

TRAVIS DIED LIKE A HERO AT AN LOC GOING BACK TO SAVE HIS BUDDIES THAT'S WHAT HIS CAPTAIN'S LETTER SAID. LIKE A REAL AMERICAN HERO.

I see my great-aunt Ginny-Mae once a year at the family reunion. She never seems to change.

I NEVER WILL FORGET, WE GOT THE NEWS THAT SAME WEEKEND YOU WERE IN THE HOSPITAL WITH WILL. LIKE THE PREACHER SAID,...

Same old stories, same good heart, and enough Final Net to stick a cat to the sidewalk,

FAMILY REUNION
By Sean Stewart and Steve Lieber

... IN THE MIDST OF LIFE, WE ARE IN DEATH.

Small Beer Press   One Dollar

Family Reunion
San Diego Comic-Con Bootleg Edition.

Sean Stewart
and
Steve Lieber

Most people think of ghosts as... vapor. Dreams.

PRESIDENT TO TROOPS: A LOT OF WORK LEFT TO DO

Houston Chronicle

They're not. They're more real than you are.

WILL, WOULD YOU HELP ME BRING OUT THE BIG ICEBOX?

"WILL?"

"ICEBOX?"

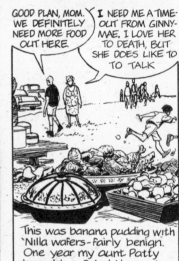

GOOD PLAN, MOM. WE DEFINITELY NEED MORE FOOD OUT HERE.

I NEED ME A TIME-OUT FROM GINNY-MAE. I LOVE HER TO DEATH, BUT SHE DOES LIKE TO TALK

This was banana pudding with 'Nilla wafers—fairly benign. One year my aunt Patty brought a Salad Nicoise in Jell-o. Swear to god.

THAT BOY OF HERS HAS BEEN WITH THE LORD THIRTY-TWO YEARS. I JUST WISH...

"...I JUST WISH SHE COULD LET HIM GO..."

DO I REMEMBER THERE WAS A COUSIN ENLISTED SAME TIME AS YOU?

YESSIR. GINNIE MAE'S BOY. HE DIDN'T ENLIST, THOUGH. HIS DRAFT NUMBER JUST CAME UP.

"SHOULD HAVE GOT A DEFERMENT. HE HAD HIM A BASEBALL SCHOLARSHIP AT AUSTIN."

HOOK 'EM HORNS

"BUT HE BUSTED UP WITH HIS GIRLFRIEND THE NIGHT BEFORE HIS EXAMS."

WHO THE HELL IS THIS GUY?

WHAT ARE YOU DOING? **SPYING** ON ME?

HEY MAN, LIKE..."HOOK 'EM HORNS!"

FAMILY REUNION (Small Beer Press)

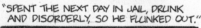
"SPENT THE NEXT DAY IN JAIL, DRUNK AND DISORDERLY, SO HE FLUNKED OUT."

"GIRLFRIEND TOOK HIM BACK BUT BY THAT TIME, THE SERVICE GOT HIM."

"HE WAS ONE OF THOSE DISCONTENTED FELLAS."

"WHEREVER HE WAS, THAT'S THE ONE SPOT HE DIDN'T WANT TO BE AT."

"SOMETHING'S WAITING UP THERE."

"IT'S NOT WHAT YOU CAN SEE COMING THAT GETS YOU..."

"...THE SERIOUS SHIT IS ALREADY THERE, SNEAKING UP ON YOU FROM BEHIND."

"COYOTE?" WHAT THE HELL KIND OF NAME IS "COYOTE?"

women is bitches

ABOUT THE TIME YOU WERE FIXING TO COME INTO THE WORLD, THE VC PUT A BIG PUSH ON AN LOC.

"THEY OVER-RAN THE CAMP WHERE TRAVIS WAS. HE KILLED ABOUT A DOZEN OF THEM WITH HAND-GRENADES, THROWING REAL HIGH HEAT."

"FINALLY GOT PICKED OFF GOING BACK TO RESCUE A BUDDY."

"GINNIE MAE FRAMED THE LETTER THAT CAPTAIN OF HIS WROTE ABOUT IT AND HUNG IT ON HER WALL."

FAMILY REUNION (Small Beer Press)

WHY'D YOU COME TO ASK, ANYWAY? DID YOU—

NAH, JUST CURIOUS.

LOOKING FOR SOMETHING?

OH, UH– I WAS JUST LOOKING FOR MEGAN. I WANTED TO GET ME SOME SUGAR FROM THAT DAUGHTER OF YOURS.

SHE'S WITH HER MOM. IT'S NOT ONE OF MY WEEKENDS.

As far as seeing dead people goes, the family and me are pretty much Don't ask, Don't tell.

I SURE WAS SORRY ABOUT YOU AND JOSIE. I DIDN'T SEE THAT COMING.

ME NEITHER.

FAMILY REUNION (Small Beer Press)

WHAT THE HELL ARE YOU LOOKING AT?

WHAT DO YOU WANT, ANYWAY?

Houston Chronic

PRESIDENT TO TROOP

A LOT OF WORK LEFT T

Longhorns

I LOOK LIKE I WORK FOR THE U.N. OR SOMETHING? I CAN'T DO ANYTHING ABOUT THAT.

OH.

Longhorns

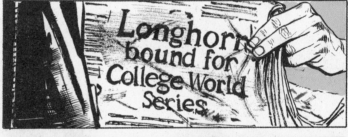

Longhorns bound for College World Series.

HOOK 'EM HORNS.

FAMILY REUNION (Small Beer Press)

FAMILY REUNION (Small Beer Press)

37.

"THANKS FOR THE SKETCH, KEV - OH, AND
THE BOOK IS GREAT! INSPIRATIONAL!"

"THINK YOU'LL GET AN EISNER?
YOU MUST BE REALLY HAPPY!"

38.

"OF COURSE YOU SHOULD VOTE FOR YOURSELF!
YOU THINK CHRIS WARE ISN'T MARKING HIS BOX?"

"C'MON, KEVIN... BE SELFISH FOR A CHANGE."

39.

"NO, MOM... THE AWARD-WINNING CARTOONIST
IS TELLING HIS SON A BEDTIME STORY."

"NO, HE DOESN'T KNOW WHAT HIS NEXT PROJECT IS.
HE'S HAD SOME OFFERS... WE'LL LET YOU KNOW."

40.

"WELL, THEY SAY THE THIRD DRAFT'S THE CHARM.
IT'S YOUR FIRST SCREENPLAY - NO BIGGIE."

"RELAX NOW... WORK ON YOUR NEW BOOK.
YOU DO HAVE ANOTHER BOOK COMING OUT, RIGHT?"

41.

"I DON'T KNOW - JUST DON'T DRAW ONE ABOUT ME!"

"I KNOW YOUR PUBLISHER WANTS ANOTHER BOOK...
BUT I CAN'T HELP YOU COME UP WITH IDEAS."

42.

"WHADDYA MEAN 'OUT OF PRODUCTION CAPITAL?'
FIND SOME! NO... DON'T TELL ME THE MOVIE'S KILLED...
OF COURSE HE'S WORKING ON ANOTHER BOOK-
THAT'S NOT THE POINT! WE HAD A DEAL."

"YOU ARE WORKING ON ANOTHER BOOK, RIGHT?"

43.

"MAYBE TAKING A BREAK TO PLAY
CATCH IS A GOOD IDEA, KEVIN."

"YOU'VE BEEN STARING AT
THAT BLANK PAGE ALL DAY..."

44.

"YOU KNOW I THINK YOUR STUFF IS BOSS, KEV...
BUT WE'VE ALLOCATED OUR PUBLISHING CAPITAL
TO DEAN AND JAMES THIS YEAR... AND AUTOBIO
ISN'T THE DRAW IT USED TO BE..."

"HAVE YOU SPOKEN TO THE LOWRIDER GUYS?"

· WE WERE NOT MADE FOR THIS WORLD ·

Sand gathers in his knee joints.

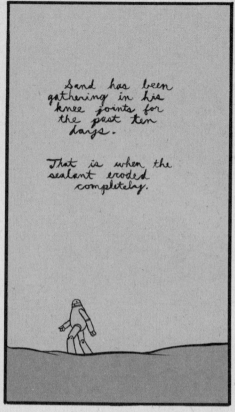

Sand has been gathering in his knee joints for the past ten days.

That is when the sealant eroded completely.

Sand gathers in his knee joints at sixteen to thirty-two granules per minute, depending on wind speed.

Eight to ten are forced out by the still functioning internal defenses...

... but clearly this leaves accumulation.

With effort he modifies his walking method, taking more abbreviated steps, allowing less exposure of the vulnerable area.

Now there is slightly less accumulation...

...but still ground is lost.

He is sharply aware he may not reach his destination.

If such a destination even exists.

WE WERE NOT MADE FOR THIS WORLD (Adhouse)

Another minute passes and another seventeen granules come in. Nine are pushed out.

He focuses on the horizon and tries to think it is beautiful.

Somewhere along this line of the horizon, he theorizes is a place where they still exist.

The things that built the Assembly and the City.

WE WERE NOT MADE FOR THIS WORLD (Adhouse)

Series and series ago, somewhere something had to have built them, or so he reasoned.

And perhaps these things would explain why they built them.

And perhaps it would explain everything.

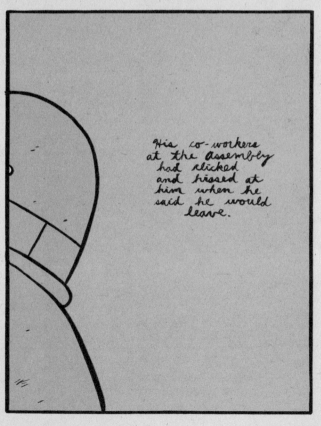

His co-workers at the Assembly had clicked and hissed at him when he said he would leave.

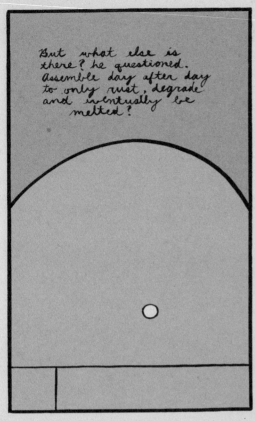

But what else is there? he questioned. Assemble day after day to only rust, degrade and eventually be melted?

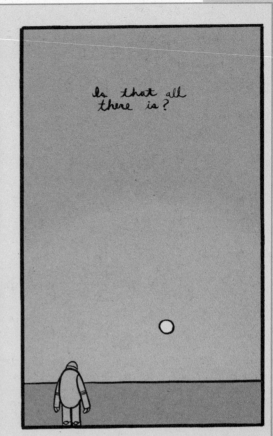

Is that all there is?

He found it impossible to accept and they found him impossible to accept.

and so he left.

Because of the sand, perhaps, he cannot bring up how long ago that exchange was. He estimates thirty days. Unknowingly, he is correct in his estimation.

Regardless, he knows it was far before the sealant, apparently ill-designed for the sand and wind of the desert outside the City, broke down.

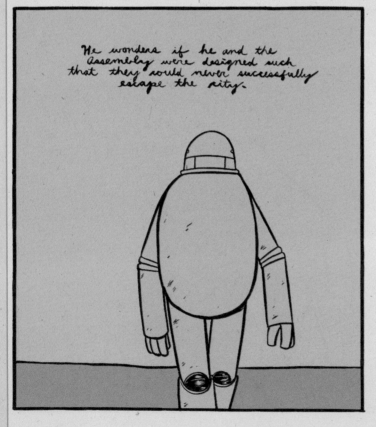

He wonders if he and the Assembly were designed such that they would never successfully escape the City.

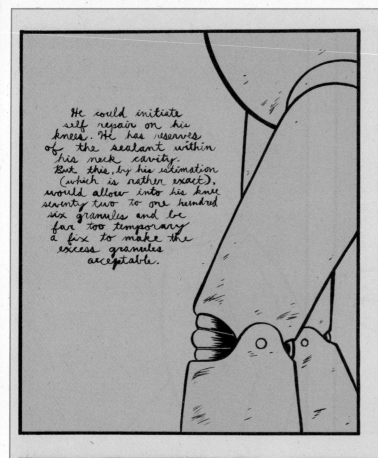

He could initiate self repair on his knees. He has reserves of the sealant within his neck cavity. But this, by his estimation (which is rather exact), would allow into his knee seventy two to one hundred six granules and be far too temporary a fix to make the excess granules acceptable.

He estimates he will not be able to walk within a week.

He continues his abbreviated steps.

He begins a diagnostic on his elbows, wondering how long his arms can carry him after his legs have failed to do so.

another minute passes

and another twenty-two granules come in.

He focuses on the horizon and tries to think it is beautiful.

Eight are pushed out.

They've been parting visitors from their money for so long here in Venice that they can't help but be good at it. Normally, they give value for money. That last encounter left a sour taste in my mouth. They didn't cheat the tourists when I came here as a boy.

And that starts me remembering once again.

I have remembered this too much; so now I can no longer be sure whether it is the event that I am remembering, or my memory of the event.

A hot, still day. Lizards, on the side of a brick wall, watch me warily.

You could catch them, if you were fast enough. But if you grabbed them by the tail it would break off, wriggling, in your hand, while the lizard ran away.

I had been staying with my aunt and uncle, with my cousins. My Italian was not good, but I could make myself understood, and we all spoke some English.

We loaded the picnic food and the bottles of fruit-juice and the wine into my Uncle's vaporetto, the water-taxi he drove, and we travelled out into the lagoon until we reached the island.

There are many islands in the Venice Lagoon. Over the years they have all been inhabited, my Uncle told me, as I proudly steered the boat. But times change. He pointed out the islands that hold factories, barracks, munitions, convents, as we passed.

I remember the slosh, slosh, slosh of the water against the side of the motorboat.

WHEN I WAS A YOUNG MAN, IN THE ARMY, WE WERE STATIONED ON THIS ISLAND. ON THE NORTH SIDE IS AN OLD MONASTERY.

NOW IS ALL RUINS. BUT IS A GOOD PLACE FOR A PICNIC.

YOU KEEP AWAY FROM THE RUINS. THEY WILL BE DANGEROUS.

YES, UNCLE.

We all ate bread and fish and fruit and chocolate. We drank apricot juice, the adults drank wine. Then my Aunt and Uncle sat beneath an old fig tree and read a book or dozed, and sent us to play, with one final warning to keep well away from any ruins.

We played hide-and-seek across the southern half of the island, clambering over ruined walls.

I grew bored with the game, or perhaps my cousins had hidden themselves too well.

I kept walking...

SANDMAN (Vertigo/DC Comics)

SANDMAN (Vertigo/DC Comics)

AT NINE IN THE MORNING, THE COUNT AROSE AND DECLARED FOR THAT EVENING A MASKED BALL OF UNPARALLELED SPLENDOR AND MAGNIFICENCE.

CASKS OF SHERRY WERE BROUGHT UP FROM THE CELLARS, ALONG WITH BOTTLES OF THE FINEST WINES.

ANIMALS WERE SLAUGHTERED AND SPITTED.

COSTUMES WERE EXAMINED, MASKS WERE PURCHASED AND REPAIRED. THE WORD WAS SENT TO VENICE, AND THE SURROUNDING ISLANDS.

AT 3:02 PM A FLOCK OF SNOW-WHITE DOVES ROSE INTO THE AIR AND FLEW ACROSS THE ISLAND.

AT DUSK, A FLOTILLA OF BOATS, EACH WITH A LANTERN IN THE PROW, PULLED UP IN THE BAY...

...DISCHARGING SEVERAL DOZEN WOMEN, MASKED AND EXQUISITELY DRESSED.

NOBLEWOMEN!

SOME WHISPERED.

COURTESANS!

SAID OTHERS.

NUNS, FROM THE CONVENT OF SAN MICHELE DI MURANO, HERE IN DEFIANCE OF THEIR VOWS...

WHISPERED THOSE WHO HAD SCULLED THE OARS.

SANDMAN (Vertigo/DC Comics)

DOES THIS VAPORETTO GO OUT TO THE ISLANDS?

IT GOES *ANYWHERE*, AS LONG AS YOU *PAY*. YOU WANT A TOUR OF THE ISLANDS?

MY BROTHER CAN MAKE YOU GOOD DEAL FOR GLASS ON *MURANO*.

I told him which island I wanted him to take me to, then described where it was to the best of my recollection.

MM. IF YOU WISH. BUT IT IS DESERTED. THERE ARE NO STORES, NO RESTAURANTS, *NOTHING* FOR A VISITOR TO SEE. AND IN THIS WEATHER...

I KNOW.

I'LL PAY.

So he took my money, and the vaporetto, the water taxi, sped through the canals of Venice on its way to the lagoon.

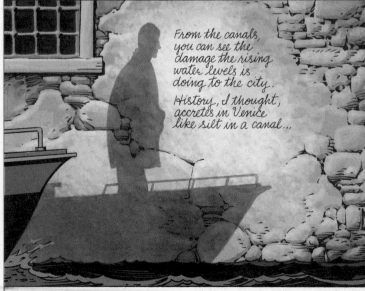

From the canals, you can see the damage the rising water levels is doing to the city.

History, I thought, accretes in Venice like silt in a canal...

...and it laps against the bricks and rocks and the deep wooden piles.

And as we ride, I find myself wondering: If my life would have been different—if, say, I had not gone to the island as a boy.

Would I have stayed with Patricia?

Would I have joined the army, applied for the unit I applied for?

Perhaps I would still be with Patricia, if, at each kiss, at every touch, I had not compared her to the woman on the island.

Her eyes were not so dark and sparkling.

Her smile was never so haunting.

I channel that longing for something I cannot reach into my job. I do it efficiently.

Someone has to.

I tell the vaporetto driver to wait for me.

HELLO. YOU CAME BACK. I THOUGHT YOU WOULD.

Everything moved slowly when I saw her. The rain seemed to fall gently, like snowflakes.

YOU KNOW, I ALMOST THOUGHT I HAD *IMAGINED* YOU.

NO. I'M REAL.

DO YOU COME OUT HERE *EVERY* DAY? OR DO YOU *LIVE* HERE ON THE ISLAND?

I GET AROUND. YOU KNOW, YOU'RE THE FIRST PERSON EVER TO COME *BACK.*

DO YOU REMEMBER WHAT YOU DID THE *LAST* TIME YOU WERE HERE?

I TRIED TO OPEN THE GATE.

WOULD YOU LIKE TO TRY AGAIN?

YOU KNOW, THERE'S PROBABLY SOME LAW PROTECTING HISTORICAL REMAINS.

I pulled. It was set fast into the brick. I was angry with myself, I thought, I should have brought a sledge-hammer, or a crowbar, or a wrecking ball.

Then I thought to kick it.

SANDMAN (Vertigo/DC Comics)

And kicking that damned gate seemed suddenly to be the most satisfying thing I could do.

I was kicking at my life.

At my family.

At my unit.

At death, at time, at every lie I had ever been told.

At every paper doll jiggling on its invisible string ...

YOU **DID** IT!

WHERE ARE WE?

MAY THE 23rd, 1751.

THAT'S A **WHEN**, NOT A **WHERE**.

HERE, IT'S A **WHERE**.

CAN YOU WAIT HERE?

I HAVE BUSINESS INSIDE.

I WANT TO COME **WITH** YOU.

OKAY, I GUESS.

YOU WANT TO BLEND IN, DON'T YOU? COME ON, LET'S SPOIL THE PARTY.

YOU LOOK MOST *LOVELY*, YOUNG LADY.

WILL YOU WALK WITH ME?

ONLY FOR A *LITTLE* WHILE, GIUSEPPE, YOU DIED OF SYPHILIS IN 1768, IN AN ATTIC IN TRIESTE.

HE DROWNED IN A STORM.

SHE DIED IN CHILD-BIRTH.

AS AN OLD MAN, HE CHOKED ON A BONE IN A BOWL OF FISH SOUP.

SANDMAN (Vertigo/DC Comics

A

AGE OF BRONZE
All contents copyright © 2004 by Eric Shanower. All Rights Reserved. AGE OF BRONZE™, Linear B, and all characters and their distinctive likenesses are trademarks of Eric Shanower. Published by Image Comics. www.imagecomics.com/

AMERICAN ELF: THE COLLECTED SKETCHBOOK DIARIES OF JAMES KOCHALKA © 2004 By James Kochalka. Published by Top Shelf Productions, Brett Warnock and Chris Staros. All Rights Reserved. www.topshelfcomix.com/

ARTESIA AFIRE
Artesia is © and TM 1999 Mark. S. Smylie. Artesia Afire is © 2004 Mark S. Smylie. The Book of Dooms is © and TM 2003 Mark S. Smylie. The ASP logo is TM 2003 Archaia Studios Press. All Rights Reserved. Published by Archaia Studios Press. www.artesiaonline.com/

ASTONISHING X-MEN
by Joss Whedon, John Cassaday and Laura Martin © 2004 Marvel Characters, Inc. Published by Marvel Comics, a division of Marvel Entertainment Group, Inc. marvel.com/

ATHENA VOLTAIRE
Athena Voltaire is a trademark of Steve Bryant and Paul Daly. © 2005 Steve Bryant & Paul Daly. Found online at www.athenavoltaire.com/

B

BATMAN
© 2003 DC Comics. All Rights Reserved. Published by DC Comics. dccomics.com/

BLACKSAD
Written by Juan Diaz, illustrated by Guarnido. Copyright © 2003 Dargaud, Juan Diaz Canales and Juanjo Guarnido. All Rights Reserved. Published by ibooks, inc. www.komikwerks.com/

BLAB 14
All stories, artwork, and illustration © copyright 2003 by the respective artists unless otherwise indicated. Published by Fantagraphics Books. fantagraphics.com/

BLANKETS
© 2004, 2003 Craig Thompson. Published by Top Shelf Productions, Brett Warnock and Chris Staros. All rights reserved.

BOMBABY: THE SCREEN GODDESS
by Antony Mazzotta. Bombaby is ™ and © 2003 Antony Mazzotta. All Rights Reserved. Published SLG Publishing. www.slavelabor.com/

BUDDHA BY OSAMU TEZUKA
© 2004 Tezuka Productions. Published by Vertical, Inc. www.vertical-inc.com/

C

CLYDE FANS
by Seth © 2004 by G. (Seth) Gallant. All Rights Reserved. Published by Drawn & Quarterly drawnandquarterly.com

COURTNEY CRUMRIN IN THE TWILIGHT KINGDOM
by Ted Naifeh. Courtney Crumrin in the Twilight Kingdom is ™ and © 2003, 2004 Ted Naifeh. Unless otherwise specified, all other material © 2004 Oni Press, Inc. All Rights Reserved. www.onipress.com

D

DEMO
Copyright © 2004 Brian Wood and Becky Cloonan. All Rights Reserved. Published by AiT/Planet Lar. ait-planetlar.com/

DOC FRANKENSTEIN
by The Wachowski Brothers, Steve Skroce, Jason Keith, Comicraft. Copyright © 2004 Burlyman Entertainment, Inc. All Rights Reserved. Published by Burlyman Entertainment. burlymanentertainment.com/

DOGS AND WATER
All contents are © 2004 by Anders Brekhus Nilsen and Airplane. Published by Drawn and Quarterly.

E

EIGHTBALL
by Dan Clowes, 2004 A.D. All Contents © Daniel G. Clowes. All Rights Published by Fantagraphics Books, Inc.

EX MACHINA: THE FIRST HUNDRED DAYS Ex Machina is ™ Brian K. Vaughan and Tony Harris. All Rights Reserved. Published by WildStorm Productions, an imprint of DC Comics.

F

FABLES: MARCH OF THE WOODEN SOLDIERS Fables © Bill Willingham and DC Comics. All Rights Reserved. Published by DC Comics/Vertigo

FAMILY REUNION
'Will Kennedy' and 'Family Reunion' are © Sean Stewart. Art © Steve Lieber. seanstewart.org/; www.stevelieber.com Originally published by Small Beer Press: www.lcrw.net/seanstewart

FAREWELL, GEORGIA: FOUR FOLKTALES TOLD BY BEN TOWLE
Farewell, Georgia is ™ and © Ben Towle, all rights reserved. August 2003. Published by Slave Labor Graphics Publishing.

THE FILTH
Copyright © 2002, 2003 Grant Morrison and Chris Weston. All Rights Reserved. Published by DC Comics/Vertigo

FINDER: THE RESCUERS PART THREE
All contents and character likenesses © Carla Speed McNeil. Published by Light Speed Press www.lightspeedpress.com

THE FIXER
by Joe Sacco © 2003 Joe Sacco All Rights Reserved. Published by Drawn & Quarterly

G

THE GOON
by Eric Powell ™ & © 2003 Eric Powell. All Rights Reserved. Published by Dark Horse Comics. www.darkhorse.com/

H

HARD BOILED ANGEL
by Hyun Se Lee English version © 2004 Central Park Media Corp. Published by CPM Manhwa, a division of Central Park Media Corporation. www.centralparkmedia.com/

S

THE SANDMAN: ENDLESS NIGHTS

SCANDALOUS

SCOTT PILGRIM SCOTT PILGRIM,

SEAGUY

SERENITY ROSE

SINGULARITY 7

SKYSCRAPERS OF THE MIDWEST

SMALL GODS

SMAX

SPOOKHOUSE

STRAY BULLETS

STREET ANGEL

SUPERMAN: SECRET IDENTITY

SUSPENDED IN LANGUAGE

T

TOMMYSAURUS REX

**A TREASURY OF VICTORIAN
MURDER: THE BEAST OF CHICAGO**

TSUBASA

TWILIGHT X STORM

U

ULTRA

W

THE WALKING DEAD

WE3

WORLD OF HARTZ

X

XXXHOLIC

Y

YOSSEL

YOU CAN'T GET THERE FROM HERE